Mixed-ability teaching
in language learning

Other CILT publications

for tutors of adult learners

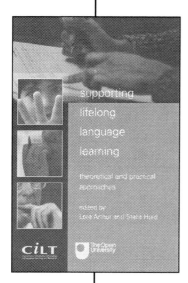

Supporting lifelong language learning
Theoretical and practical approaches

Ed. Lore Arthur & Stella Hurd

In association with The Open University

This book supports tutors in meeting the rapidly changing demands and expectations of learners in post-compulsory education. It will provide a tool for professional and personal development; offer guidance on classroom approaches; advise on skills development and learner strategies; help with preparing for accreditation; enable tutors to make the most of computer-mediated language learning; and offer guidance on interpreting policy requirements in the professional context. The book is intended for a wide audience of FL, CL and EFL tutors.

Understanding language learning and learners • Approaches to learning and teaching • Technology • Assessing progress • The professional context

240pp   1 902031 45 8   £15

DIY techniques for language learners

María Fernández-Toro & Francis R Jones

This book gives practical information, ideas and techniques to learners who are teaching themselves a foreign language, to teachers who want to support their students' independent learning, and to advisers who work in self-access centres. Part I provides advice on general approaches and principles of independent learning and presents a series of questionnaires to help individuals discover their own language learning profile. Part II offers guidance and DIY techniques for developing specific language skills and areas, i.e. vocabulary, grammar, reading, listening, writing, speaking.

The detailed discussion of independent language learning, together with in-depth guidelines on learning styles and the wide range of practical techniques make this an indispensable handbook for anyone learning on their own, or those supporting or advising independent learners.

Part I: Getting started • You as a learner • Preparing to learn • Getting started • Diagnostic questionnaires • Part II: DIY techniques • Vocabulary • Grammar • Reading • Listening • Writing • Speaking • Alphabetical list of techniques.

144pp   1 902031 46 6   £15

Mixed-ability teaching in language learning

Susan Ainslie and Susan Purcell

CILT
Centre for Information
on Language Teaching and Research

The views expressed in this publication are the authors' and do not necessarily represent those of CILT.

Acknowledgements

We would like to thank Noemi Rivera-Leon, PGCE trainee teacher at Edge Hill, for the activities in Spanish, and Ute Hitchin of CILT for her guidance, support and helpful comments.

First published 2001 by the Centre for Information on Language Teaching and Research (CILT) 20 Bedfordbury, London WC2N 4LB

Copyright © Centre for Information on Language Teaching and Research 2001

Illustrations by Dandi Palmer

ISBN 1 902031 53 9

2005 2004 2003 2002 2001 / 10 9 8 7 6 5 4 3 2 1

A catalogue record for this book is available from the British Library

Printed in Great Britain by Copyprint UK Ltd

CILT Publications are available from: **Central Books,** 99 Wallis Rd, London E9 5LN. Tel: 0845 458 9910. Fax: 0845 458 9912. Book trade representation (UK and Ireland): **Broadcast Book Services,** Charter House, 27a London Road, Croydon CR0 2RE. Tel: 020 8681 8949. Fax: 020 8688 0615.

Contents

Introduction

Aims of this book

The cornerstone of successful teaching is the ability to meet the widely differing needs of the individuals within the groups we teach. This is a particular challenge for the tutor in Adult Education because groups may include learners at different levels with widely different previous experiences, expectations, aspirations and needs. It is important for the tutor to be able to manage such a group successfully, so that the needs of all the individuals in the class are met.

Adult Education tutors are usually already dealing with mixed ability to some extent, even if they are not aware of doing so. There are strategies they can adopt and resources they can use or adapt without too much preparation which will enable them to do it more often or more effectively. This book aims to help tutors to meet this challenge and includes suggestions for:

- identifying the needs of the individuals within a group;

- getting learners in the same group to work with different texts;

- giving learners tasks at different levels based on the same text;

- conducting whole group oral work in a way which caters for the different needs within the group;

- managing group work effectively;

- using Information and Communications Technology.

This book updates and expands on *Netword 3: Mixed-ability teaching: Meeting learners' needs*. It is divided into three parts: Part 1 sets the context, defining 'mixed ability' and giving an overview of ways of planning for differentiation, and of key principles and strategies. While Part 1 incorporates examples as illustration, Part 2 consists of the description of activities which can be used at each of the three key phases of a lesson, for presentation, practice and consolidation. Guidance is given for each activity on how to set it up and then follow it through, and what the linguistic outcome will be. Reference is made throughout Part 2 to the photocopiable resources in Part 3 which can be incorporated in the activities as described, or adapted for other purposes.

Many of the resources can be used as they are for any language, but where appropriate, examples are provided in English, French, German and Spanish.

Part 1
Rising to the challenge

Chapter 1: What is 'mixed ability'?

Mixed ability is a shorthand term to describe a whole range of interrelated differences between the individuals in any group. The term includes the literal definition, i.e. learners with **a varying capacity for language learning**. This may be innate – an ability to recognise patterns, to remember new vocabulary or to imitate sounds – but it may also relate to previous experience of language learning. The 'beginner' who has already learned a foreign language, for example, is likely to pick up a second foreign language much more rapidly than the learner who is new to language learning; a degree of linguistic awareness and language-learning strategies will probably already be in place.

Learners come to classes at **different levels and with different strengths and weaknesses.** They may previously have learned at another evening class, at school, from a television series, or while living in the country where the language is spoken. They may have good grammatical knowledge but not much experience of speaking; they may be good orally but have difficulty with writing. They may have a broad vocabulary but have difficulty understanding the spoken word. A 'beginners' class usually includes genuine beginners and 'false' beginners who may have studied the language at school; a beginners' class in one Romance language may include learners who are already fluent in another Romance language and who will therefore tend to pick up the new language very quickly.

Progress made in learning a language is, however, dependent on a complex combination of factors in addition to those related specifically to language learning. Before we move on to consider what the tutor can do to optimise learning, let us consider other factors within the learner or the learning context which may facilitate or impede progress.

Why do learners attend class?

Reasons for attending classes are many and varied and have been documented in more detail elsewhere (see Units 1 and 2 of *The adult language learner* (Arthur and Hurd, eds, 1992) for a more comprehensive review of the motivation, interests and needs of adult learners). The reasons may be related to learning a language *per se* but may also be personal or professional. They include:

- **for work-related purposes** either in a job the learner is already doing, or to improve chances of promotion/a new job;

- **to make new friends;**

- **to have an evening out on a Tuesday;**

- **to keep the mind alert;**

- **for holidays;**

- **to be able to communicate with friends/relatives;**

- **to get a qualification;**

- **for pleasure;**

- **to learn about the culture and way of life;**

- **to help their children at school.**

Reasons for attending may also change during the course. For example, something to do on a Tuesday may turn into an interest in learning the language once the course is under way.

Effective Adult Education tutors try to find out as early as possible which of the above apply, so that they can design their course programme appropriately.

Factors which affect progress

It has long been recognised that the most important factor in language-learning success is **motivation**, and in Adult Education classes motivation is usually high, though the motivation of one learner may be very different from that of another. And motivation may dip or increase as the course progresses.

People have **different learning styles** (*The adult language learner*: 46): some need visual input, a lot of adults 'like to see it written down'; some like to work on their own; others need the support of a group. Some prefer to work in pairs; others want the constant attention of the tutor. Some are happy if they can understand the gist of what is being said; others feel insecure if they do not understand every word. Learners will come to classes with preconceptions about what the class should be like: some will want a formal approach, others are happy to work in pairs and groups. Some become anxious if the work presented to them includes a lot of language with which they are unfamiliar; others welcome the challenge. These factors also need to be taken into account by the tutor.

6

Learners who have already succeeded in the educational system or who have a successful professional background are likely to feel confident that they can succeed in language learning. They will probably have developed study skills, whereas those with limited **previous educational experience** may well have little idea how to go about learning. On the other hand, a manager in the same class as a clerical assistant may find it difficult if the office junior is better at learning the language than he or she is. If the learners' previous experience of education has not been happy or if they have a background of unemployment, they may suffer from low self-esteem and worry that they may not be able to cope. Women with children and carers, who have not been employed recently, tend to fall into this category.

Other factors, no less significant, play a role in the learners' progress. Older learners (who are **not** too old to learn) may need a different approach, as their short-term memory becomes less 'elastic' once they reach their fifties. It is particularly important to progress in short steps and to give older learners the chance to absorb new material before moving on. Any specific learning difficulties, such as visual impairment or deafness, have to be taken into consideration, as do the varying external pressures on our learners – young children, demanding jobs, problems at home, tiredness on arrival at the class and so on. Some learners will come to our classes not having opened a book since the previous class, while others may have been studying every day. How can we even attempt to present them with a lesson which will be at an appropriate level for all? (Ainslie, *Mixed-ability teaching: Meeting learners' needs*, pp2–10, discusses the nature of 'mixed ability' in more detail.)

Implications for the learner

In any Adult Education class learners will find themselves in a group which includes a mixture of the above, even if their centre offers classes at a range of levels in any one language. Indeed, in a climate of cuts and cost-effectiveness, it may well be that the number of levels is restricted, particularly in less common languages, and that the differences in levels between learners are therefore considerable. How will the learners feel and how will they cope?

Adult Education class members tend to be characterised by an initial lack of confidence. Learners joining a class for the first time are likely to feel a degree of anxiety; they may find 'the old hands', used to the world of Adult Education, intimidating. Their anxieties will probably be based either on fears about their own performance or on factors relating to what the course is going to be like. For example:

- the fear that they do not know as much as the others in the group and may look and feel stupid;

- concern that they may not be able to learn;

- a worry about taking on the unfamiliar role of the learner, maybe for the first time in many years, when they are used to being in control;

- shyness joining a group of people they do not know in an unfamiliar environment;

- uncertainty about what the course holds for them, about what they have let themselves in for;

- suspicion when the teaching approach of the tutor may be different from what they remember at school;

- worry as the class proceeds that others in the class seem to be picking things up more quickly than they are.

It is for the tutor, aware of the anxieties mentioned above, to allay these fears. The learners have elected to join a course, in spite of their worries, and the support of the rest of the group, as well as appropriate support and guidance of the tutor, will help them to achieve their potential. It is important for the tutor to discuss with learners sympathetically any concerns and anxieties they may have and to be prepared to discuss approaches to and content of the course.

Implications for the tutor: the need to differentiate

Dealing with the large number of factors identified above would appear to be a huge task. There are, however, a number of ways in which teaching can be approached in order to ensure that we are taking them all into consideration. This is not to infer that every activity and all resources will meet the needs of all the individuals in our classes, but rather that in every lesson (usually two hours in Adult Education plus 'homework') the needs of all the members of the group will have been addressed. (See Appendix 1, p89, for an example of a two-hour lesson.)

The term normally used to indicate that we are addressing 'mixed ability' is '**differentiation**'. It affects all aspects of the teaching/learning process, and has been defined as:

'*... the process by which curriculum objectives, teaching methods, assessment methods, resources and learning activities are planned to cater for the needs of individual pupils*' (*Modern Foreign Languages in the National Curriculum*, DFEE, 1992, Section E. The definition is just as applicable to adult learners, if not more so.)

Differentiation can be achieved in a number of ways, and the way we choose will depend on the make-up of the group we are teaching and also the objectives of a particular unit of work. Approaches to differentiation can be divided into three broad categories:

- the way we organise and manage our classes (see below);

- the way in which we respond to and encourage our learners, irrespective of what we happen to be teaching at any time (see Chapter 2);

- lesson content and methodology: differentiated learning objectives, tasks or texts (see Chapter 3).

Planning for differentiation

When we introduce learners to new language, we usually follow the logical progression of:

1 **presenting** new language to the learners;

2 **practising** new language, i.e. the learners try it out;

3 **consolidating** the new language by giving learners the opportunity to use it in a freer, less structured way.

The starting point of any lesson is its **objectives,** i.e. what we want the learners to be able to do at the end of the lesson that they could not do at the beginning. This is clearly problematical if we are trying to meet the wide-ranging needs identified above, as the different members of the group will have different personal objectives.

It is not practicable or desirable to give all the learners different things to do throughout a lesson. The learners have opted to join a group and want the benefit of the support of that group and the social interaction which a group provides. There is, however, a way of approaching many lessons which makes it possible to allow for the needs of each individual in the class. This is to identify objectives and content into three groups:

Core	What everyone ought to be able to do.
Reinforcement	Additional exercises that some learners will do in order to have more practice and more time allowed to reach the core objectives of the lesson.
Extension	Different or more challenging exercises for those who have grasped the core objectives and are capable of extending their knowledge, developing their expertise or who have specific individual needs.

These three phases are identified in the Non-Statutory Guidance for the National Curriculum for Modern Foreign Languages for schools, but are equally applicable to any age group. In teaching new material and the likely mode of delivery, they fit into the above model as follows:

Phase of lesson	Type of objective	Mode of delivery
Presenting new language	**Core**	**Whole class**
Practising new language	**Core** **Reinforcement**	**Whole class** **Pairs/groups** **Individual**
Consolidating	**Reinforcement** **Extension**	**Pairs/groups** **Individual**

This will clearly not be adhered to in every lesson, as it would become tedious and learners would become all too aware of where they fitted into the levels of the class, but it is one manageable way of differentiating between individuals within a group.

Planning a topic

It is usually easier to incorporate a differentiated approach into our teaching if we start at the planning stage, when we prepare an overview of how we intend to approach a topic. The following is an example and suggests ways in which the different levels and needs of the individuals in a group can be addressed at every stage of the teaching process. The topic below generally arises early on in the course, but it is assumed that some key vocabulary will already be familiar to the learners, e.g. *bonjour/s'il vous plaît/merci/au revoir/monsieur, madame, mademoiselle, c'est combien,* some numbers. Learners may need to be reminded of some of these, and numbers will certainly need revising regularly. The topic will take two or three lessons to work through, depending on the group, with revision at the beginning of each lesson.

Level I	**Aim:** To enable learners to get themselves something to eat and drink when in a (French)-speaking country
Topic: *In a café bar*	

Core objectives

By the end of the topic **all learners** will be able to ask for something to eat and drink and pay for it. **Some learners will:**

- be able to ask for a greater range of items;
- have additional specific vocabulary according to their tastes;
- be accurate in use of gender;
- be able to use several expressions to ask for items.

Content (core)	*Opportunities for differentiation*
1 Introduction to topic and key new vocabulary (basic items of food and drink – eight to twelve items in total depending on group and level of response). (Possible list: *un café, un thé, un vin rouge, un vin blanc, une bière, un hot dog, une pizza, un sandwich au jambon, un sandwich au fromage, une glace, des frites* – very common vocabulary with a number of cognates.)	Before giving learners new vocabulary, ask the class to give vocabulary they may already know.
2 Presentation and repetition of key new vocabulary with flashcards/objects, etc. (Add *vous désirez, je voudrais* here after initial presentation and practice.)	After choral repetition, ask better learners to produce the new vocabulary first, so that they can act as models for the others. • Encourage more able learners to produce longer utterances than the others. • Correct with sensitivity according to the level of the learner.
3 Listening comprehension exercise – dialogue in a bar. (Prepare by revision of '*c'est combien?*' and numbers practice and consolidation.)	Give learners choice about how they address the exercise, e.g.: (a) they will probably have a list of vocabulary either on the board/in their books/on a handout – suggest that if they don't need to, they could try to do the exercise without looking at the list; (b) prepare two listening exercises, one asking for boxes in a grid to be ticked (see Activity 10, p40), one requiring written responses in the language. If both exercises are on one handout, the choice can be made without learners drawing attention to themselves; c) alternatively, have an extra box at the end of the grid to give the opportunity for learners to add additional information.
4 Correction of listening exercise.	If correcting in class, ask easier questions of learners who may find more difficult questions challenging – save the difficult questions for more advanced learners. Write the answers on the board or OHP so everyone can check.
5 Reading comprehension exercise, e.g. a menu and a short dialogue in a café (see Activity 13, p 45).	Have additional exercises for those who finish quickly, e.g. more than one menu, longer dialogue, with more vocabulary. Exercises should normally be graded in degree of difficulty – easier ones first. All learners will complete earlier exercises, but only some will do later ones.

Content (core)	Opportunities for differentiation
6 Role play; in a bar, in pairs. Structured tasks based closely on new vocabulary introduced.	Have a list of key expressions at the bottom of the role-play sheet, but suggest that if they can the learners fold it over and do the role play without consulting the list **or** Give more than one role play and learners progress through them or choose the one(s) they would like to try. Consider strategies when putting learners into pairs, e.g. same level together **or** putting learners together so that one can help the other. Tutor gives support by moving round group.
7 Feedback from role play.	Some pairs may be keen to 'perform' their role play in front of the rest of the class – others may be too inhibited to try. For these you could listen to them and give feedback while the rest of the group is still preparing. With enough encouragement they may in time become less inhibited about 'performing' in front of the others. Correct sensitively at the end of the exercise – picking up on key recurring errors without singling individuals out for correction.
8 Revision/recall of vocabulary; introduction of additional lexical items. (e.g. *c'est tout, un café crème, un café au lait, un jus d'orange, de l'eau, un verre de, une bouteille de, pression, qu'est-ce que c'est, une menthe à l'eau?* Introduce alternatives to *'je voudrais – avez-vous?, est-ce que je peux avoir?'*.)	Try to elicit vocabulary first, then negotiate additional expressions, e.g. ask learners if they have other drinks/snacks that they would particularly like to be able to ask for. Include cultural awareness here (e.g. describe *un croque monsieur, un citron pressé, un kir*, different prices at the counter and on the terrace, the aperitif.)
9 Listening/reading comprehension to practise wider range of vocabulary.	As in 3, 4 and 5 above.
10 Video clip of café/bar with associated tasks.	Some learners might need a handout of key vocabulary; others may be able to understand without extra help.
11 More complex role plays – in groups. Authentic/more extensive stimulus material (menus).	Some may need an alternative task, e.g. to repeat the basic role play in a pair; others may now be able to order a wider variety of items, to order for their friends and to ask for further information. Tasks could be more open-ended and, where appropriate, learners could be encouraged to develop them as they wish.
'Homework'.	This may be learning vocabulary/preparing role plays/reading comprehension exercises. Discuss with learners how they might approach learning independently and develop study skills. Encourage them to be involved in making decisions about what will be the most useful type of activity for them. Learners could be encouraged to design menus for one another to use as stimulus material – preferably produced on computer. Or they may be able to find 'authentic' menus on the Internet. They may also already have menus from trips abroad that could be brought in for the group to use.

Dealing with beginners/non-beginners

Although there will inevitably be a mixture of levels in any class, the necessity of dealing with beginners and non-beginners in the same class is a particular challenge. It is a situation that tutors often have to deal with, although non-beginners may not admit to having some prior knowledge, either at enrolment or at the beginning of the course. Indeed, non-beginners sometimes claim to be beginners and their true level only becomes apparent as the class proceeds.

If a class has been advertised as a beginners' class, then the tutor's priority must be to make sure that real beginners are catered for; there is a danger that the non-beginners may hijack the class and the real beginners fall behind and quickly feel demoralised. As a tutor it is easy to ask questions, get answers from a small number of learners in the group, and assume that everyone understands, whereas in fact some may be feeling quite lost but do not have the confidence to say so. Tutors need to guard against this in all their teaching and to make sure that all learners are being regularly monitored to check the learning that is taking place.

It is good practice to talk to the group about the fact that there are learners at different levels within it, and to discuss how you are going to approach the teaching in order to cater for everyone's needs. It could also be pointed out that there are potential advantages, e.g. the more advanced learners may be used as models when new language is being introduced, and they may be able to work with the real beginners from time to time and give them additional help. It is important to make sure that the beginners do not feel that they are somehow inferior because they are at a lower level, and at the same time that there will be occasions when you will be providing more challenging work for the more advanced learners. From time to time the level of language heard in the class may be quite advanced for the beginners, but there is no harm in their being exposed to the natural patterns of the language, as long as you have told them in advance that this may be the case. It may indeed be possible for them to gain something from it, to understand additional information. In practice, as the class proceeds, the differences of level will probably be gradually eroded as other factors, such as innate language-learning ability or amount of time spent studying between lessons, come into play.

The plan outlined earlier of core, reinforcement and extension is a good standard pattern for a class of beginners/non-beginners. Even if the core work is already known to the non-beginners, there is no harm in some revision. Opportunities can be built into the class to ensure that all learners have work at their own level.

An initial lesson might include some of the following:

- Share objectives with the class – core objectives are that by the end of the lesson all members of the group will be able to say what their name is, where they live and where they come from, but that some learners may be able to give more information, for example to talk about their families, their jobs and hobbies.

- In introducing the key structures, elicit them where possible from the group rather than simply telling them what they are.

- Ask non-beginners to give the same information about themselves as the tutor has just presented, as a basis for comprehension questions.

- Prepare listening and reading comprehension tasks at different levels, or encourage learners to add additional information. Have extra ones available which include more wide-ranging content.

- For pairwork have handouts available but encourage learners not to refer to them if they don't need to.

- Give open-ended tasks towards the end of the lesson, e.g. give a brief talk about yourself/write about yourself. These tasks can be performed at any level.

- Before introducing a writing activity, ask learners if they know any of the orthographical differences between English and the language of the class before you give them this information.

Dealing with beginners/advanced learners

Tutors are sometimes faced with a group which includes a very wide range of learners, e.g. from beginners to A level standard. This situation is more likely to arise with less commonly taught languages, and the option may be either to try to run the class or to have no class in the language at all. If possible, a class like this should be avoided and it should be brought to the attention of those responsible for organising Adult Education provision that it is a very difficult situation for the tutor and often less than satisfactory for the learners. Alternatives could be sought, such as one Adult Education centre liaising with another to offer two viable classes between them at different levels, or one class running at two different levels in alternate years.

If, however, tutors find themselves faced with no alternative but to run such a class, a more radical approach may have to be adopted. A two-hour class could be split into two halves, one half with the tutor 'teaching' one of the groups while the others work through tasks set by the tutor (or chosen by the learners with the tutor's guidance) individually or in groups, and the second half the other way round. It would generally be preferable for the beginners to be taught in the first hour, as they will need initial input from the tutor before they can be left to work through exercises on their own or in groups. The advanced learners in the first hour could be preparing work from stimulus material (listening or reading texts) prepared by the tutor. To support the 'self-study' part of the lesson, IT resources could be particularly useful. There are, for example, some good interactive CD-ROMs available and there are language exercises available on the Internet with instant feedback (see Appendix 3, p97, for suggested websites).

Needless to say, the learners will not fit neatly into two groups, but it would be very difficult to divide them into more than two basic groups, in each of which it will be necessary to differentiate on occasions. From time to time it would be a good idea to bring the two groups together, e.g. to show one another work or role plays that they have prepared, for the more able to be paired with the less able, for a simulation which will involve the whole group with roles at different levels according to ability.

It may be possible for the two groups to work to a similar theme or topic, e.g. travel and transport/expressing opinions/the environment/health; if so, maybe the more advanced group could prepare work for the lower level to use in class. Or maybe they could do some research to find out about an aspect of the topic which they then explain to the rest of the group.

EXAMPLE 1. Health. The advanced learners are given reading materials or websites which explain how the health service is organised in France/Germany/Spain and how foreign tourists gain access to health care; meanwhile the beginners are learning parts of the body, how to say what's wrong with them, how to make an appointment at the dentist's, etc. When their research is completed, the advanced learners give a presentation to the others on the outcome of their preparatory work – in English or the target language or a combination of both according to the level of the other group.

EXAMPLE 2. Travel and transport. The beginners learn how to buy tickets and make travel arrangements. They then prepare a role play at the travel agents. The advanced group meanwhile finds out about travel and transport in the country concerned, either from material provided by the tutor or by exploring the Internet, e.g. by visiting webpages produced by various tourist destinations. In the final part of the lesson the two groups come together for the role play; the advanced learners work at the travel agent's and the beginners have to make reservations.

This approach requires a lot of thought, time and imagination on the part of the tutor, and it would therefore be a good idea for tutors to get together to pool ideas and resources and produce joint schemes of work.

It will be very important at the beginning of the course for the tutor to discuss the strategy being adopted with the learners, so that everyone is clear about what is being done and why. Though the demands on the tutor in terms of preparation and organisation will be considerable, the resulting class could be very stimulating and a lot of fun.

Chapter 2: Preparing the ground

Establish the right atmosphere

From the very beginning of the course it is important to establish a supportive, friendly atmosphere that will encourage learners to relax and to feel comfortable with the tutor and also with the rest of the group. Then they will hopefully be prepared to discuss their individual needs and interests, which the tutor will need to know in order to plan to meet them. Learners need to feel valued and that, if they do not do as well at times as some of the others or get things wrong, it does not matter. They need to feel that it is alright for them to want to do something different from time to time.

We should take care with the content of our early lessons in case they are pitched at too high a level or the learners do not understand what they are expected to do. We do not want them to feel anxious, embarrassed or threatened. Sometimes there are one or two learners in a group who tend to dominate and they can be very off-putting for others, so we need to do our best to make sure that everyone has the same opportunity to participate. Getting learners working in pairs or small groups is one way of reducing this problem; getting to know everyone's name early on helps us to direct questions specifically at named people so that it is not always the same one or two who answer. Some of the strategies mentioned below should help to get the group on the right track.

Get to know your learners

If tutors are to organise their classes in such a way as to be able to meet the needs of the different learners in a group, as discussed in Chapter 1, they need first to get to know them. There are a number of ways in which to begin to do this, and the earlier it starts the better.

- Try to be available at enrolment to discuss the course and the learners' needs.

- You may wish to ask them to complete a simple questionnaire, either before the course or at the first lesson (see sample questionnaire in Appendix 2, p96). This should not be too long or complicated or learners will not want to complete it.

- Ice-breaking activities can also help you to get to know them, e.g. for intermediate learners: 'Talk to someone in the class you do not know, in the foreign language, and then tell the rest of the group about him or her.' For advanced learners: 'Talk to someone in the class you do not know and find out three things you have in common and three things you do not have in common.' An activity like this will give you information about linguistic competence and also personal information about the members of the group. It will also indicate the level of confidence or anxiety of the learner when speaking in front of everyone else.

- Keep notes about the learners as you build up a picture of them.

- Discuss with the learners how you are approaching the course, the fact that they are all different, will not have the same previous language-learning experience and may have different things they want to get out of the course. Explain how you are planning to organise your classes to enable all of them to meet their own needs.

- Discuss with the learners how they might go about studying, how they might have different preferred ways of learning and that they should reflect on their past experience in this regard. Involve them in the whole learning process; this will probably make your job easier.

■ Give learners choices about what they would like to do. This will encourage them to play an active part in the learning process.

Start small

Having got to know your learners, the next step is to focus on how to set about meeting their different needs. However, it takes us all – tutors and learners – time to get used to approaching something in a different way. It is unwise to embark upon a complex activity until you and the learners have had experience of a more straightforward differentiated task.

Initial approaches to differentiation do not require major changes to the way we operate. A first step could be to look at our existing lesson plans and try to identify in each lesson one activity which provides an opportunity for differentiation. Examples of activities which are straightforward to manage are:

■ a worksheet which has a couple of extra, more challenging, exercises added on at the end for those who finish before the others and would like to try them;

■ a true/false exercise in which those who can write the correct version of the false statements;

■ a grid for completion as a listening exercise which has an optional extra column for 'additional information', anything that the learner can understand that is not covered in the other columns (see Activity 15, p52);

■ a gap-filling exercise in two versions: one with the words to go in the gaps at the bottom of the sheet in the wrong order, and one with no words given. A variation of this would be to have an OHT (overhead transparency) prepared with the words on (or write the words on the board), but suggest to the learners that they try to do the exercise first without looking at the transparency.

Chapter 3: Strategies

Having prepared the ground, we need to incorporate a range of strategies into our lessons in order to ensure that we meet the diverse needs of the learners in our groups.

Language level

The key ways to differentiate in terms of language level are:

1 **By text.** This means that we use different texts with different individuals or groups within the class. Texts include any stimulus material, ranging from reading materials, listening materials to role play stimulus materials, etc. For example:

- two different reading passages for the class, one easier than the other;

- worksheets which include a number of exercises which progress from easier to more difficult, with the expectation that not all learners will manage to complete all the exercises;

- two listening passages dealing with different topics, e.g. one a conversation on holiday and one a business meeting;

- roles in the same role-play activity which are at different levels of difficulty, e.g. one has the key expressions to be used given on the cue card, one does not; one has to act as the chair at a meeting and others are only required to speak occasionally;

- learners doing exercises to practise different skill areas or aspects of the language according to need, e.g. some doing a grammar exercise, some watching a video, some practising oral work, some working on the computer.

2 **By task.** This means that the whole class is working on the same stimulus material but doing different exercises to exploit it. A straightforward example would be a worksheet which requires gaps to be filled in. One sheet has the answers given (though in the wrong order) at the bottom of the page, and one does not. A Cloze test (in which every nth word is missed out) can be easily differentiated by giving one group the passage to complete with every eleventh (say) word missed out, and one group every seventh word missed out. This can be done with a click of the mouse on the *Fun with Texts* computer package. (See p22 for guidance on using *Fun with Texts*.)

3 **By outcome.** This simply means that everyone is given the same task but that what is produced is different. Writing a letter is one example of this; oral question and answer often produces different responses. This is the sort of differentiation that happens anyway. We need to evaluate the tasks we set our learners and make sure that from time to time an exercise is sufficiently open-ended to allow 'differentiation by outcome' to take place. If we only ever give gap-filling exercises, or structured role plays which do not allow for creativity or originality on the part of the learner, we are limiting the extent to which we are differentiating.

4 **By level of support.** Some learners need extra support, more time spent going over exercises, giving more guidance, explaining again what the rest of the class understood first time. They may need extra handouts, e.g. paradigms of verbs, lists of key lexical items. We must not, however, focus on the weaker members of the group to the exclusion of the more advanced ones; they too may need extra support in the form of, for example, more advanced reading texts to work on by themselves. As tutors we must

try to help all our learners to achieve their full potential. Learners also need different levels or types of psychological support: some need a lot of praise, reassurance and encouragement to allay their anxieties and build up their confidence.

5 **By time.** Some learners may need more time to complete an activity or to grasp a new concept or to learn new lexical items.

Other factors

The choices we make about the activities we incorporate into our lessons are not only centred on linguistic considerations. Other aspects of our teaching which may not immediately appear to have anything to do with teaching mixed ability in fact play a part in ensuring that we meet the needs of all our learners.

Variety

Learners learn in different ways, have different needs and aspirations, different learning styles and different strengths and weaknesses. In order to meet the needs of such a diverse group it is important to build variety into our lessons, though this variety should of course be within a coherent whole and a lesson should demonstrate progression. This variety could include the following:

■ introducing new language in several different ways before moving on to practice activities, e.g. visual stimulus via flashcard or OHT, repetition from the visual stimulus without explanation, grammatical explanation, asking learners to deduce patterns, written stimulus, use of translation;

■ work at different levels at different times of the lesson;

■ different skills – a mixture of listening, reading, speaking, writing – preferably in each lesson (which may include homework);

■ different resources, materials and media, e.g. video, CD-ROM, authentic materials such as magazines or brochures, textbook exercises, handouts,

■ different types of activity – from structured to unstructured, teacher-led to independent, those requiring little learner input to those requiring a lot of learner input (e.g. gap-filling or letter-writing), from grammatical to communicative;

■ different classroom organisation – plenary, pairwork and group work, work undertaken individually.

By including a wide range of the above, we are more likely to find ways of meeting the needs of all. And again, by discussing with our learners and asking them to evaluate the effectiveness of different strategies we may find that for one group certain methodologies are preferred.

Short, manageable chunks

Those learners with an earlier experience of failure in education have probably joined a course with some trepidation. It is extremely important that such a feeling should not be repeated; early success is vital. Setting learners manageable tasks and short-term goals so that they can see that they are making progress is important if you are not to lose them. Lesson by lesson and even task by task learners must be aware of their learning objectives, must be set a task that is within their capabilities, and what they have achieved afterwards must be clear to them. Early success will boost confidence and can be built on as the course proceeds.

We need to introduce new material in short segments so that older course members and slower or less advanced learners have the time to assimilate it before moving on to something else. As there will be a range of levels within a group, this can best be managed by dividing the class into groups from time to time.

Plenary oral work

This is an area of teaching mixed ability that most of us do automatically without appreciating that it constitutes an important part of a differentiated approach to teaching.

- Visuals such as flashcards or overhead transparencies can encourage the production of language at many levels.

- When introducing new language we may want to ask more advanced learners if they can produce it first, as they may already have some knowledge of it.

- When doing practice question/answer we can ask questions at different levels of difficulty depending on the learner being asked. The table below gives examples of different types of questions, gradually progressing from simple to complex. While the normal pattern when introducing a class to new language would be to progress more or less in order through the list, if a group is very mixed in terms of ability you may find it more appropriate to vary this pattern. It can be seen that in the earlier examples very little is required of the learner beyond repeating and then understanding.

From simple to complex	
Tutor activity	**Learner response**
1 Tutor shows pictures and says new words. Choral and individual repetition. (e.g. *he is getting dressed, brushing his teeth, having his breakfast, etc.*)	Repeat after tutor.
2 Tutor holds up picture and says: *he's getting dressed or he's brushing his teeth*	Learner selects one of statements and repeats it.
3 True/false activity. Tutor holds up picture and makes a statement, which may or may not be what is on the picture.	Learner says true or false.
4 Teacher puts all of pictures on board and says one of the sentences being practised.	Learner points at correct picture.
5 Tutor holds up picture and asks: *what is he doing?*	Learner must reproduce sentence from memory.
6 Tutor asks learners what they do in the morning. Notion of time may be added.	Learner must change verb form and be able to reproduce sentences.
7 Tutor asks learner what he did this morning.	Learner must change verb form and tense and be able to reproduce sentences.

- We can expect more or less in terms of the answer given according to our knowledge of the learner – some may have done very well if they produce a simple three-word statement, others we might want to encourage to produce a more complex sentence including a subordinate clause.

- We can make decisions about the extent to which we correct the learners according to their level.

- Some learners may feel too shy to say anything at all – and we should not force them, but perhaps encourage them to have a go either individually or in a small group at a different time in the lesson.

Group work

Getting learners to work in pairs or groups has a number of advantages:

- the groups may work at different levels or speeds, by design or as an activity develops;

- learners are less likely to feel inhibited to speak than when in a whole class situation and may feel confident to ask the teacher or one another questions;

- the teacher can help individuals or groups or work with one group at a higher level;

- the learners have more opportunity to practise;

- the class will become less teacher-centred;

- overbearing learners will only be able to dominate one small group at a time;

- working in a group can encourage the learners to develop interpersonal and communicative skills and the ability to work as part of a team – and also helps them to get to know one another.

There are, however, one or two techniques to adopt which will help to ensure that group work is effective:

- discuss with the group the benefits of working in smaller units – some learners are not convinced of its value and complain that they are only hearing the imperfect language of the other learners; they may also not have experienced this sort of class organisation before and expect a teacher-led approach;

- make sure the language to be used has been thoroughly practised beforehand and that learners are clear about what their task is, or the group may tend to revert to English;

- limit the amount of time spent in a group activity – or the task may be forgotten;

- form groups in a variety of ways, sometimes chosen by the learners and sometimes by the tutor; to be always in the same group can get very tedious. To form groups you may:
  - put learners of the same level together; sometimes they can be unhappy about always being in a lower level group, however, so try to avoid labelling, and be tactful and sensitive to their feelings;
  - put learners in interest groups to work on a topic that may not be of interest to the whole class;
  - put stronger learners with weaker ones, to give them support;
  - select randomly, by number, colour, etc;

- go over group work afterwards in a plenary, to discuss issues that may have arisen and to check what has been done.

Encouraging independence

It is a very good idea to encourage our learners to be independent of us, to develop autonomy and to take responsibility for their own learning. We do not want them to stop learning when our course is over and we do not want them only to be able to learn when in our class or doing our 'homework'. There are many resources for foreign language learning available to all learners nowadays, including a range of good quality coursebooks, videos and audio-tapes, multi-media television programmes, CD-ROMs, computer packages, up-to-date information, games and interactive sites via the Internet, and of course the range of resources that our learners can pick up on foreign travel as it becomes more and more affordable for all. Learners are usually only too delighted to bring in brochures from places they have been to abroad for use by the class or material they have been sent by friends abroad. They can be encouraged to develop a bank of resources for use by the class, and occasionally time could be set aside for independent work with these materials. Many colleges have a language centre which could be used for a similar purpose. Thus independent learning could take place in the classroom as well as outside it. The more learners feel involved in and in control of the learning process the more effective that process is likely to be, and learners will be able to take control of their own differentiation by choosing what they do.

Error correction

The correction of errors should be handled with sensitivity according to the objective of an activity and the individual concerned. It is a general principle of teaching that learners should be given positive encouragement and that achievement should be rewarded with praise. A few years ago it was felt that the communication of a message was the only thing that mattered and that errors that did not interfere with this should be ignored. Linguists who have been taught using this approach and who have subsequently decided that they want to be teachers are now facing the problem that they have never been taught to use the language accurately, and they have to learn the grammatical structure of the language in order to be able to give a correct model to their students.

It is now generally recognised that learners should be encouraged to be as accurate as possible so that they at least have the opportunity to achieve their full potential, while at the same time not forgetting that the prime objective of the ability to speak a foreign language is to be able to communicate with others. (See Purcell, *Teaching grammar communicatively*.) Mark schemes and approaches to error correction should reflect this, and should be shared with the learners. Separate marks can be awarded for communication of a message and for accuracy, and the interpretation of a mark scheme will depend on the individuals concerned and the need to ensure that learners are not discouraged.

Errors being made by several learners within the group can be corrected with the group as a whole rather than with individuals. Errors that are being made by an individual rather than a group should be dealt with in a quiet moment with that individual and not in front of the whole group. A learner who produces an answer with an incorrect gender or word order, can be helped to put it right if the tutor says, for example – '*Très bien – mais, **un** bleu voiture???*' If an exercise produces answers with a lot of mistakes in it, a tutor might not have prepared it adequately or might have pitched it at an inappropriate level. If this happens, the tutor may decide that it is most appropriate to ignore certain errors and to concentrate on the key ones. No-one learns very much from a piece of paper covered in red ink.

The potential of Information and Communications Technology (ICT)

What is IT?

You will come across two acronyms when talking about using information technology, ICT (Information and Communications Technology) and IT (Information Technology). ICT is the term recently introduced to reflect the expanding functions of what is now available to us with emphasis on communication as much as on the transmission of information. For our purposes, however, there is no need to be concerned about any difference.

It is often assumed that ICT/IT refers only to the use of computers, but it is, in fact, more wide-ranging than that and includes all the media, from cassette recorders to the overhead projector (OHP), to television and video, in addition to the wide range of functions now available to us via the computer. This section focuses on the potential of computers, but examples of the other media in use are included among the activities and resources provided in Part 2 and Part 3 of this book.

Sometimes tutors and learners alike are reluctant to use a computer, but it has tremendous potential for language learning. There is now a computer in over 60% of homes and the number is increasing all the time. Thus more and more of our learners will have a computer at home, and this has implications for what we are doing. If the tutor does not have access at home, it should be possible to gain access via the Adult Education centre.

Potential for the tutor

Tutors can use computer-based resources in a number of ways to enhance the quality of their teaching and introduce variety to meet the different needs of different learners:

- Preparing high-quality handouts which can be kept and re-used or easily adapted from year to year – and for purposes of differentiation.

- Improving the quality and impact of presentations by incorporating pictures and visual symbols for flashcards, handouts, etc – there's no longer any need to be able to draw! ClipArt or other similar packages provide thousands of pictures which can easily be incorporated into a handout.

- Accessing language-learning packages for use with our classes, either bought or available via the Internet, which enable learners to work at their own pace and often give instant feedback.

- Access to a wealth of resources on the Internet.

- Helping with administration as lists are so easy to generate and to modify.

Potential for the learner

Computer-based resources can also enhance the quality of the learning experience for the learners in a number of ways, both inside and outside the classroom. These may be summarised as independence and choice. For example:

- greater independence from the tutor: working at their own pace with instant feedback from the computer;

- the opportunity to repeat exercises several times if necessary – without feeling embarrassed or anyone getting impatient!;

- the possibility of choosing which exercises they will do;

- a way of introducing variety into learning;

- access via the Internet to an endless bank of resources.

The down side

Clearly the computer is not without its problems. At college we are all familiar with computers crashing just at the very moment when we need to print off a vital document; if we work on more than one computer or with more than one package, it may not be possible to transfer from one to another or at the very least the layout will probably be affected. We have all 'lost' work or wasted a lot of time trying to get our machines to function as we would wish; and the experts we call upon to help us may appear to be speaking a foreign language which we cannot understand, and we can feel that we are very stupid.

Sometimes technology is not the best or most appropriate way to meet our learning objectives, so we should not use it without reflection on what we are hoping that the learners will learn. The technology may interfere with the learning of the language.

Another danger for those of us who do have some basic computing skills is that we can spend hours searching the Net for some good resources and not find anything suitable at the end of it all. There are also a lot of poor websites which will not be of any use; anyone can put an exercise on the web. Make sure that the pages you choose to use are useful and contain no mistakes. (See the list of websites on p97.)

Another problem can be the attitude of some tutors and learners, a fear of something that is unknown. In the twenty-first century, however, we cannot ignore the computer and will need to get over this fear; it is worth investing in a computer for home use and in a course to develop basic computing skills. Such courses should increasingly be available via the Adult Education centre. It is also worth investing some time in practising because it does take time getting to grips with what has to be done. And most colleges will provide tutors with access to computer technicians who can give help, as well as to booklets which give instructions in how to use different features of the computer.

In our classes it is unlikely that there will be no-one able to use a computer; those who are reluctant to try could perhaps be paired up with someone who can help them. And often there is someone in the group who will be delighted to help the tutor who gets into difficulties.

tips

1 Always save work onto a floppy disk and label the disk.

2 Follow instructions exactly or it will probably go wrong.

3 Make sure you get website addresses exactly right, including dots, or the computer will not recognise them.

4 If you make a mistake and lose a document, use the 'undo' icon at the top of the screen – it will take you back to where you were.

5 Always have a plan B ready for when the computers/the video recorder/the cassette player don't work in class or are suddenly not available.

6 If you find a good website make a note of it for future reference – and start with the list of suggested websites given at the end of the book. Use Bookmark: you will see a bookmark icon on the menu at the top of the computer screen while on the Internet; just click on it and it will save the document into your own folder so that you can find it again easily.

7 If you find you are not sure what to do from the screen in front of you try scrolling down the page – the icon you need to click on may be at the bottom of the page out of sight.

8 Be aware of copyright regulations. Many newspapers and magazines do not allow you to use their copy.

9 When downloading from the Internet you may have difficulty with pictures or other images – they will probably need to be saved separately from the rest of the document, and sometimes they cannot be downloaded at all.

10 Try out something new before the class, just to be sure.

11 Enlist the help of learners to hunt for good resources and websites at home.

12 Don't give up – you can do it and it will enhance the quality of your teaching!

things to do

1 Encourage learners to get into a foreign language website – e.g. Yahoo France/ Germany/ Spain and make **e-mail** contact via chat-lines.

2 Find out how to do **accents** in the foreign language – either via the symbol icon or by using alt and number keys – given via the help icon.

3 Try a **text manipulation package** (e.g. *Fun with Texts* or *Storyboard*). The tutor types in text and the package allows the learner to choose to do a range of activities, e.g. Unscramble words, unscramble lines, predict what the text will be, etc. Many colleges will have a copy of this package, and the instructions are relatively straightforward to follow.

4 Type in the name of a town in the country of the language you are teaching, and see what sort of information this produces – it may be maps, guides to hotels, timetables, information about shopping, general **tourist information** – really useful for teaching resources. You could also ask your learners to do the same.

5 Explore the **BECTA (British Educational Communications and Technology Agency)** website (see Appendix 3, p97). This website gives invaluable guidance on a range of issues related to language teaching, including suggestions for ways of exploiting *Fun with Texts* (see, for example, *Twenty Activities that Work.*) Examples of other documents are CD-ROM reviews, numerous information worksheets, whole class pedagogy, and so on.

6 Explore the website produced by Hull University (see Appendix 3, p97) – which is an excellent gateway to language learning resources.

7 Lingu@NET was established by BECTA and CILT and offers expert advice and information for language teachers and learners (see Appendix 3, p97).

Part 2
Classroom activities
Teacher's notes

This part consists of a range of activities which exemplify the strategies outlined in Part 1. Throughout this section reference is made to the relevant photocopiable resources (**R#**) in Part 3 of the book. These resources are indicated to the right of the activity title to which they apply.

For ease of access the activities are divided into three sections, **Presentation, Practice and Consolidation,** as discussed in Part 1 (see p7). In practice the activities do not always fit neatly into one of the sections but may be used in slightly different ways in more than one phase of the lesson.

Chapter 4: Presentation activities

Activity 1 • Directions around town

R1 R2 R3

Language practised

Asking for and giving directions; describing where places are using prepositions (opposite, past, next to, etc).

Type of activity

Whole class.

Resources

Basic street plan (see **R1**), plus whichever overlays (**R2** and **R3**) are appropriate for the level of your class.

Preparation

Prepare the basic street plan (see **R1**) on an OHT. If you think that your class can cope with more than just the basic 'turn right/left, go straight on', prepare an overlay with additions to the map (**R2**) that will allow you to present 'take the first/second/third on the left/right', 'carry on to the traffic lights/end of the road/square', 'go past the station/traffic lights/over the river'. It is best to start off with a very basic street plan containing a few roads and not much else, rather than have everything on one OHT. In this way the same basic OHT can be used at different stages throughout the course or even with classes at diffferent levels, with overlays added to practise the language being taught at the time.

Cut two long strips from an OHT and draw a figure of a person on the end of one and the symbol of a car at the end of another (see below). If your language has different words for 'to go' depending on whether you mean on foot or by a vehicle (c.f. *gehen, fahren*), you can swap between both strips to practise both verbs.

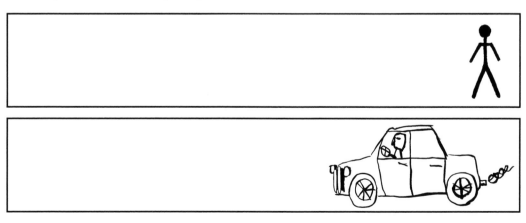

For practising the use of prepositions, prepare a third overlay (see **R3**), showing symbols of various buildings seen around town – cinema, church, etc. If your language is inflected, you might want to restrict where you position each symbol so that you are only using prepositions governing just one particular case. Where other prepositions are needed, other symbols can be added on a fourth overlay. The more overlays you use, among which a specific amount of information is split, the more flexible your resources will be.

Procedure

1 Show the basic OHT (**R1**). Hold one of the long strips at the blank end and 'walk' the person around the street plan, saying 'turn right' as your 'person' turns right and so on. Ask learners to think up an appropriate question, e.g. 'where is the theatre?', 'is there a chemist's shop near here?' to make the giving of directions a bit more realistic, as well as to get them involved.

2 Back up your explanations with gestures and illustrations around the classroom or college building – use directions to a place everyone knows – the toilet, or canteen, for example – to ensure comprehension.

3 When you have had sufficient practice of each structure, add an overlay to practise another few phrases or another structure. Do not feel obliged to cover all the language mentioned here; it may well be that you have a gap of several weeks before you introduce prepositions, for instance.

4 Get learners to join in with you as you say out loud the directions. Gradually say less and less, leaving the learners to give the correct directions based on what you are doing with the strip of acetate depicting the pedestrian or car.

When you are happy that learners have understood and can produce the phrases correctly, you are ready to move on to a practice activity (see p28 in this book for a follow-on activity).

Activity 2 • Presenting the news (audio or video)

Language practised

Past tense, extending vocabulary.

Type of activity

Whole class.

Resources

Audio or video tape recording of a very recent news broadcast.

Preparation

Record a news broadcast just before (e.g. the evening before) your lesson. It is preferable to record a World Service broadcast, or at least a summary of international news, so that learners will be familiar with the stories and proper names mentioned.

Watch or listen to the broadcast yourself several times, making sure you are thoroughly familiar with the content. Jot down any key words for your own benefit during the lesson.

Prepare handouts depending on learners' requirements and on how much time you wish to spend on exploiting the broadcast, e.g.:

■ containing vocabulary only;

■ a full transcript of parts or all of the broadcast;

■ a gap-filling exercise based on the transcript;

■ comprehension questions or grids.

Procedure

1 Have a fifteen- or twenty-minute warm-up session, before playing the broadcast, during which you brainstorm the group's knowledge of current news stories. Ask them to anticipate what they are going to hear on the news broadcast you are about to play.

2 Accept all answers, regardless of whether they appear in the news item or not. However, if a learner mentions a topic that does appear in the broadcast, probe more deeply to elicit key words that will be heard on tape and to ensure that the basic background to the story is understood. For instance, a learner may say the word 'earthquake'. Ask questions like:

Where was the earthquake?	Le tremblement de terre, il s'est passé où?
When was it?	Il s'est passé quand?
How high on the Richter scale did it reach?	Il a atteint quel niveau à l'échelle de Richter?
How many people died?	Combien de personnes sont mortes?
How many people were injured?	Combien de personnes ont été blessées?
How many people are missing?	Combien de personnes manquent?
How many bodies have been found?	On a trouvé combien de morts?
What damage has been done?	Quels sont les dégâts?
Which countries are helping in the rescue operation?	Quels pays aident dans l'opération de sauvetage?
How are they helping?	Quelle sorte d'aide ont-ils offerte?

Do not ask all the questions just for the sake of it. Only ask those questions which will aid comprehension of the news broadcast. Write up key words as they are mentioned.

3 Play the tape for the first time and give the class just one of the following tasks:

■ ask which of the news items that were brainstormed during the warm-up period are actually mentioned in the broadcast; or

■ give learners a list of words to tick if they are mentioned; or

■ ask learners to jot down which countries are mentioned; or

■ ask learners to jot down proper names mentioned; or

■ ask learners how many news items in total are covered.

4 If you have a weak group and the broadcast is not too long you can play it a second time before checking the answers.

5 Play the tape again, this time setting another of the tasks – more challenging if the class can manage it.

6 Able learners will not become bored if you play the broadcast several more times, provided that, each time, you set another, slightly more difficult task, so that they are listening for different things. They may also be able to cope with gap-filling exercises and comprehension questions.

Weaker learners, who find the earlier tasks difficult enough, can try and complete those same tasks with each listening. Tell the group that they do not need to do all the activities, but to concentrate on the tasks at their level. If you give gap-filling or other handouts to the whole class, then go over the answers with the whole group, no-one need know which learners did not do the exercise.

Chapter 5: Practice activities

Activity 3 • Directions around town

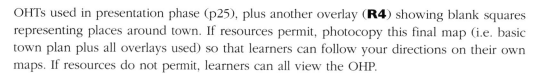

This activity follows on from the presentation activity on p25.

Language practised

Asking for and giving directions; describing where places are using prepositions (opposite, past, next to, etc) – as presented in Activity 1 on p25.

Type of activity

Whole class. Pairwork.

Resources

OHTs used in presentation phase (p25), plus another overlay (**R4**) showing blank squares representing places around town. If resources permit, photocopy this final map (i.e. basic town plan plus all overlays used) so that learners can follow your directions on their own maps. If resources do not permit, learners can all view the OHP.

Preparation

As a minimum, teach 'where is ...?' or 'how do I get to ...?', plus turn right/left, go straight on, using Activity 1 as a guide.

Procedure

1 Keep the OHP switched on using the same map plus overlays as in the presentation phase of the lesson. Add the overlay showing the eight blank boxes representing buildings around town (**R4**), which should fit neatly on to the master plan (**R1**). Mark an X on the plan to show where each set of directions begins from.

2 Ask learners to ask you the way to anywhere at all – it is up to them. Weaker students can stick to simple vocabulary, e.g. 'where is the cinema/ restaurant/ park, etc?', but more able learners can ask their way to more complicated destinations if they know the vocabulary, e.g. the dry ski slope, the open-air swimming pool.

3 When the first learner asks a question, e.g. 'where is the cinema?', direct the class, starting from X to one of the eight blank boxes on the plan. Learners trace the route on their own map and write 'cinema' next to the appropriate blank box. If you have not provided photocopies of the plan, number each box on the OHT so that learners can jot down the number of the box you have directed them to, e.g. cinema – no. 3. Make sure you tell them to make a note of where each place is, so that they can take part in the second phase of the activity.

4 Continue, with learners asking directions to different places, until you have directed them to all eight boxes.

5 Now swap roles, so that **you** ask the same eight questions that the learners did (you will need to have jotted down which box corresponded to which destination) and have a volunteer from the class direct you. Trace the route indicated by the learners'

instructions on the master plan on the OHP so that learners can check whether they got the right answer or not.

Variations

■ Rather than asking the whole class to repeat the directions you have just given, as in point 5, divide the class into pairs and let each pair check whether they followed your instructions correctly, each partner taking it in turns to ask and give directions, based on the information they wrote down at stage 3. They can compare their jottings on their maps to check their comprehension of your earlier instructions.

■ To make learners work a bit harder, have ten or twelve boxes on map overlay (**R5**) but let learners ask directions to only six or eight places. Learners then have to listen very carefully and understand more detailed instructions, such as 'it's on your right' or 'it's at the end of the road'.

Activity 4 • Dice and 'miniflashcards' | R6 | R7 |

Language practised

Verb endings, any tense.

Type of activity

Pairs or small groups (of three or four). Suitable for groups of similar ability.

Resources

One die per group, with each face showing a different personal pronoun (*je, tu, il, nous, vous, ils*) to cover all verb endings. Special dice can be purchased (see MLG Publishing details in Appendix 3, p97) or you can make your own – write each pronoun on a small sticky label and stick over each face of the die. Each pair or group needs a stack of small cards illustrating various verbs. These can be hand-drawn using stick figures (see examples below), photocopied from p68 (**R6**) or bought from the company MLG Publishing which produces attractive, coloured versions.

| **to play football** | **to dance** | **to throw** |
| *jouer au football* | *danser* | *jeter* |

See **R6** for a full set of photocopiable cards.

Preparation

Stick to one tense. More able learners may be able to cope with cards depicting a variety of verbs, e.g. those taking *être* or *sein,* reflexive or separable verbs, but otherwise stick to verbs of one type. If you want to give the class intensive practice of, say, reflexive verbs, then every flashcard can illustrate such a verb, e.g.:

to get up
se lever

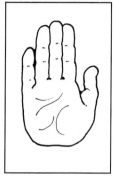

to stop
s'arrêter

to go for a walk
se promener

See **R7** for a full set of photocopiable cards.

During the presentation phase of the lesson, when you introduce or revise the particular tense, ensure that you include those verbs which are represented on the flashcards. Ideally use the same symbols or diagrams for each verb, so that learners will recognise it when they pick up a small card. This is easy to do if you have hand-drawn your 'mini cards' yourself using stick figures – just enlarge these drawings for larger flashcards for whole class use, or copy them on to an OHT.

Procedure

1 Give each pair or small group one die and a small stack of miniflashcards (placed face-down). The flashcards can be distributed at random, or if you have a weaker group you can give them a pile containing more straightforward verbs, or containing those verbs that you want them to concentrate on.

2 Learners take turns throwing the die and picking up a card. They must conjugate the verb in the appropriate person, so if '*vous*' is uppermost and they pick up a card depicting the verb 'to eat', they must say out aloud '*vous mangez*'.

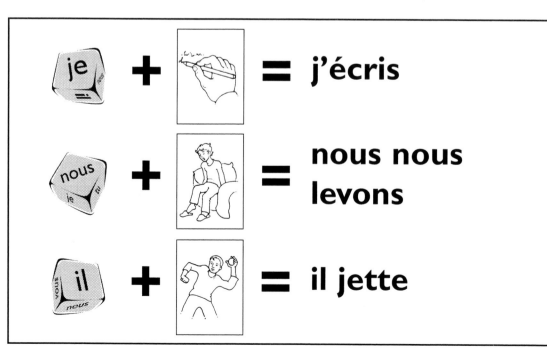

Alternatively, to avoid embarrassing individual learners by putting them on the spot, let anyone in the group have the chance to answer on each throw of the die.

Encourage learners to correct each other.

3 When group members are happy with an answer, the next person takes a turn.

4 When the pile of cards is finished, it can be turned over and used again – chances are, this time it will have to be conjugated using a different pronoun. In this way, it does not matter whether different pairs or groups work at different speeds. If you do not have many cards in total, groups can swap piles amongst themselves to have the opportunity of putting endings on a different set of verbs.

5 Finish the activity after about five or ten minutes. It is fairly intensive and challenging and best used as a short, sharp exercise. It does not matter how many cards have been turned over in total; slower groups will have gained just as much benefit as faster ones.

Variations

- Adapt piles of cards to suit the particular tense or type of verb you wish to practise. If you want the class to practise the *passé composé*, but you have not yet introduced those verbs which take *être*, you will need to remove the verbs *aller, tomber, descendre, monter*, etc from the pile you may have been recently using to practise the present tense.

- Ask learners to make up a whole sentence or form a question using the verb on the card and the pronoun thrown on the die.

- If you want to highlight time expressions, these can be included, e.g.:

  Je me lave tous les jours.
  Il regarde la télévision deux ou trois fois par semaine.
  Nous nous promenons rarement dans le parc.

Activity 5 · Nagging spouse

Language practised

Passé composé with object pronouns (in French).

Type of activity

Pairwork, suitable for pairs where one partner is weak and the other strong.

Resources

A cue card listing a number of household chores for each learner.

| faire la vaisselle |
| faire les lits |
| dépoussiérer les meubles |
| passer l'aspirateur |
| repasser les chemises |
| nettoyer les vitres |
| acheter du pain |
| poster la lettre à grand-mère |

Preparation

You will have been practising positioning the object pronoun correctly in the past tense. If you have not got beyond '*le*', '*la*' and '*les*', do not use the final two examples in the sample cue card on the previous page (*acheter du pain* and *poster la lettre à grand'mère*) as they require '*en*' and '*lui*'. Think of more examples using direct objects instead. If you have not discussed with your class past participle agreements, ensure that the pronunciation of the past participles of the verbs you have used is not affected by the preceding pronoun, as it would be if you included the examples '*écrire la lettre*' and '*mettre la table*' (*je l'ai écrite* and *je l'ai mise*).

Procedure

1 Set the scene and allocate roles. A nagging spouse (the weaker partner) has asked his or her long-suffering husband or wife (the stronger of the pair) to do various chores around the house. The latter has done only half of them. Tell the partner playing the role of the hen-pecked spouse to tick just four of the chores on their list which they have done – they haven't done the other jobs they were meant to! Make sure that the other partner cannot see which of the chores have been ticked.

2 The nagging spouse asks about all the chores on the list, making questions in the past tense:

> *Est-ce que tu as fait la vaisselle?*
> *Est-ce que tu as fait les lits?*   etc.

The other partner replies according to whether he or she has ticked or crossed the phrase:

> *Oui, je l'ai faite.*
> *Non, je ne les ai pas faits.*   etc.

The person playing this role has to use the correct object pronoun and put it in the right place, which explains why this role is more suitable for the stronger partner.

Variations

- For stronger groups include sentences which require the use of more pronouns, e.g.:

  > *aller au supermarché (j'y suis allé)*
  > *acheter des cigarettes (j'en ai acheté un paquet)*
  > *envoyer la lettre au directeur (je la lui ai envoyée)*

- For business French classes change the context so that instead of a spouse asking about household chores, the roles of boss and secretary are used:

> annuler la réunion avec Mme Dupont
>
> réserver la meilleure table
> au restaurant Chez Nico
>
> envoyer les brochures à notre filiale
>
> finir/écrire les lettres
> (aux nouveaux clients)
>
> téléphoner à M. Renard
>
> acheter les billets pour
> mon voyage d'affaires
>
> demander des brochures de notre filiale
>
> faire réparer le télécopieur

■ The examples chosen for the French task all require the use of object pronouns. If this activity is to be used in German, the German teaching point should be borne in mind when devising examples. The activity could be used to practise the past tense of separable verbs:

abwaschen	*Hast du abgewaschen?*
Mutter anrufen	*Hast du deine Mutter angerufen?*
die Möbel abstauben	*Hast du die Möbel abgestaubt?*
den Tisch abwischen	*Hast du den Tisch abgewischt?*
staubsaugen	*Hast du staubgesaugt?*
die Gäste einladen	*Hast du die Gäste eingeladen?*

Activity 6 · Asking for personal information

Language practised

Asking open questions to elicit personal information, such as:

What is your name?
Where are you from ...?
How old are you?
How many ...?
When are you ...?
What do you ...?

Type of activity

Pairwork, suitable where one partner is stronger

Resources

Cue card A and cue card B (see **R8** in French, German and Spanish).

Preparation

In the examples given, a knowledge of different tenses is required, but cue cards can be designed so that they reflect the language to be practised. Ensure that you practise the form you want learners to use during the activity, e.g. if you want them to ask 'when were you born?' rather than 'what is your date of birth?', make this clear.

Procedure

1 Distribute the cue cards so that the stronger learner receives card A. Remind them not to look at each other's card.

2 Set the context: you are on a plane approaching Heathrow. Partner A volunteers to help B whose written English is not very good.

3 Partner A is to ask the questions to elicit the appropriate answers. Partner B replies following the details given on cue card B. Partner A fills out the 'landing card'.

Variations

Any sort of 'form filling' activity is usually ideal for a pair of mixed ability because one role, that of questioner, is usually more complex. A very weak Partner B can often just read more or less what is written on the card, a more able Partner B can elaborate on the basic information given. Suitable contexts are:

R8

33

■ The hotel reception desk   ■ The job centre

Nom _ _ _ _ _ _ _ _ _ _ _ _ _ _ _ _ _ _

Prénom _ _ _ _ _ _ _ _ _ _ _ _ _ _ _ _

Adresse _ _ _ _ _ _ _ _ _ _ _ _ _ _ _ _

Nationalité _ _ _ _ _ _ _ _ _ _ _ _ _ _

Date du départ _ _ _ _ _ _ _ _ _ _ _ _ _

Nom _ _ _ _ _ _ _ _ _ _ _ _ _ _ _ _ _ _

Prénom _ _ _ _ _ _ _ _ _ _ _ _ _ _ _ _

Adresse _ _ _ _ _ _ _ _ _ _ _ _ _ _ _ _

Age _ _ _ _ _ _ _ _ _ _ _ _ _ _ _ _ _ _

Travail actuel _ _ _ _ _ _ _ _ _ _ _ _ _

Travail désiré _ _ _ _ _ _ _ _ _ _ _ _ _

Qualifications _ _ _ _ _ _ _ _ _ _ _ _ _

Nachname _ _ _ _ _ _ _ _ _ _ _ _ _ _ _

Vorname _ _ _ _ _ _ _ _ _ _ _ _ _ _ _ _

Adresse _ _ _ _ _ _ _ _ _ _ _ _ _ _ _ _

Nationalität _ _ _ _ _ _ _ _ _ _ _ _ _ _

Abreisetermin _ _ _ _ _ _ _ _ _ _ _ _ _

Nachname _ _ _ _ _ _ _ _ _ _ _ _ _ _ _

Vorname _ _ _ _ _ _ _ _ _ _ _ _ _ _ _ _

Adresse _ _ _ _ _ _ _ _ _ _ _ _ _ _ _ _

Alter _ _ _ _ _ _ _ _ _ _ _ _ _ _ _ _ _

Aktueller Beruf _ _ _ _ _ _ _ _ _ _ _ _

Angestrebter Beruf _ _ _ _ _ _ _ _ _ _

Qualifikationen _ _ _ _ _ _ _ _ _ _ _ _

Apellido _ _ _ _ _ _ _ _ _ _ _ _ _ _ _ _

Nombre _ _ _ _ _ _ _ _ _ _ _ _ _ _ _ _

Dirección permanente _ _ _ _ _ _ _ _ _

Nacionalidad _ _ _ _ _ _ _ _ _ _ _ _ _ _

Fecha de salida _ _ _ _ _ _ _ _ _ _ _ _

Apellido _ _ _ _ _ _ _ _ _ _ _ _ _ _ _ _

Nombre _ _ _ _ _ _ _ _ _ _ _ _ _ _ _ _

Dirección _ _ _ _ _ _ _ _ _ _ _ _ _ _ _

Edad _ _ _ _ _ _ _ _ _ _ _ _ _ _ _ _ _

Trabajo actual _ _ _ _ _ _ _ _ _ _ _ _ _

Trabajo deseado _ _ _ _ _ _ _ _ _ _ _ _

Cualificaciones _ _ _ _ _ _ _ _ _ _ _ _

The 'B' cue cards can be designed to take into account the learners' abilities and interests. Produce several variations so that the pairs can swap roles or can swap cue cards with another pair.

Activity 7 · Shopping

Language practised

Avez-vous …?/ Est-ce que vous avez …?
Donnez-moi …
Je suis désolé(e), nous n'avons pas de …
Du, de la, des, etc.

Fruit, vegetables, food items, etc. Any vocabulary can be practised merely by producing different flashcards and shopping lists.

Type of activity

Whole group activity.

This is a 'differentiation by text' activity. The shopping lists vary in difficulty. A weaker student can be given a shopping list (such as example A) which contains easy vocabulary and nothing more taxing than grammes, kilogrammes or litres. A more able student can be given a more varied shopping list (such as B), which requires more thought.

Resources

Four or five small flashcards (**R9**) for each member of the group. There can be duplicates in the whole set, although each individual should be given cards which differ from one another. A shopping list for each member of the class. Everything written on a shopping list should have a matching flashcard circulating.

Preparation

Ensure that the vocabulary which appears in the lists has been covered during the earlier part of the lesson. However, not all learners need to be able to produce all the vocabulary items. Perhaps produce a handout containing all the vocabulary, which learners can refer to, if they need a word.

Work through a model dialogue which may be followed during the group activity. Use an OHT sequence (see Activity 13, p45, and prepare something similar, just changing the drink items). Learners will frequently need to apologise for not having a particular item during the activity, so make sure that phrases like 'I'm sorry, we haven't any … .' are included.

Procedure

1 Give each learner a shopping list (**R9**). A weak learner could handle list A which has straightforward vocabulary and quantities. A stronger learner could manage list B. Ensure that learners can ask for what is on their list. If they don't know a particular word, prompt them.

2 Give each learner four or five flashcards representing the items to be bought. Ideally these flashcards should not depict items that are on the learner's own list, otherwise he or she will not need to ask for them, but otherwise they can be distributed at random.

3 Learners move round the class, approaching anyone who is free to ask if that person has got one of the items on their list. If the 'shopkeeper' has the relevant flashcard, the pair conduct a typical shopping conversation and the shopkeeper hands over the flashcard.

4 In this activity learners play the role both of customer and shopkeeper simultaneously. They will therefore practise more relevant language structures.

5 The activity can either continue until everyone has 'bought' the items on their list, or it can stop when there is a 'winner' i.e. the person who is the first to collect all the items on his or her list.

Note that weaker students are not being excluded from learning more difficult vocabulary. When playing the role of shopkeeper they will be approached for a jar of jam or pot of yoghurt. But they will not be asked to remember or produce this vocabulary just yet. They can practise vocabulary and expressions of quantity at their own level.

Variations

■ Vary the items on the flashcards and shopping lists to reflect whatever topic you are teaching at the time. For instance, all the items on the lists could be clothing, of different sizes and colours.

■ Add prices to the cards to encourage learners to ask about cost.

Activity 8 · At the bank

Language practised

Phrases used when changing money in a bank, e.g.:

I'd like to change/buy ...	*Je voudrais changer/acheter*
Cash or credit card?	*Des espèces ou une carte de crédit?*
What is the rate of exchange?	*Quel est le cours du change?*
It's ... to the pound	*C'est ...*
Could I see your passport?	*Je peux voir votre passeport?*
Could you sign here/there, please?	*Voulez-vous signer ici?*

Type of activity

Pairwork, graded tasks. Roles A and B are straightforward and roughly equal, except that in the fourth conversation the bank clerk is allowed freedom in how to deal with a potential problem.

Resources

A cue card (**R11**) for each learner, one person in each pair receives an A card, the other a B card.

Preparation

Demonstrate a model dialogue (similar to Conversation 1 below) with the whole group. Ensure that the meaning of all the symbols is understood. Learners will gradually get accustomed to symbols if you introduce them gradually as new phrases are taught. Some symbols will be used for several different topics, such as passport and signature, so learners will soon assimilate them.

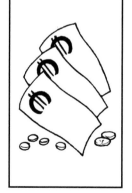  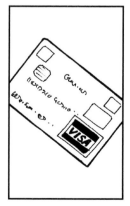

See **R10** for a full set of symbols.

Procedure

1 Distribute the cue cards. Partner A plays the role of the customer and B is the bank clerk. Tell learners not to look at each others' cards.

2 B begins by greeting the customer. Both partners then pursue the conversation by following the prompts on their cue cards. Remind pairs to take one prompt at a time; this will ensure that the conversation sounds like a realistic exchange of questions and answers, rather than a monologue.

Conversation 1 (R I I) will sound something like the following:

Customer:	I'd like to change $100, please.	Client:	Je voudrais changer $100, s'il vous plaît.
Clerk:	Certainly, cash or credit card?	Employé:	Bien sûr. Vous avez des espèces ou une carte de crédit?
Customer:	Cash. What is the rate of exchange?	Client:	Des espèces. Quel est le cours du change?
Clerk:	$1.56 to the £.	Employé:	Une livre coûte $1.56.
Customer:	Here you are.	Client:	Ça va. Voilà.
Clerk:	Thank you.	Employé:	Merci.

Conversation 4 (R I I), which is more complex and more open-ended and thus suitable for the stronger members of the class might sound like this:

Customer:	I'd like to buy 950 francs, please.	Client:	Je voudrais acheter 950 francs, s'il vous plaît.
Clerk:	Certainly, cash or credit card?	Employé:	Bien sûr. Vous avez des espèces ou une carte de crédit?
Customer:	Credit card. What is the rate of exchange?	Client:	Une carte de crédit. Quel est le cours du change de sterling?
Clerk:	8.78 francs to the £.	Employé:	Pour une livre, on reçoit 8F78.
Customer:	Is there a commission charge?	Client:	Est-ce que vous prélevez une commission?
Clerk:	Yes, one per cent. Can I see your passport please?	Employé:	Oui, un pour cent. Je peux voir votre passeport, s'il vous plaît?
Customer:	Oh dear, I've left my passport at the hotel.	Client:	Oh là là, j'ai laissé mon passeport à l'hôtel.
Clerk:	Oh, I'm afraid I can't help you then	Employé:	Je regrette, mais je ne peux pas vous aider alors.
	or		**or**
	Well, have you got an identity card?		Ben, est-ce que vous avez une carte d'identité?
	or		**or**
	How far away is the hotel?		Votre hôtel, c'est loin?
	or		**or**
	I'll need to speak to the manager in that case.		Alors, il me faut parler avec mon chef.
	etc.		etc.

3 Weaker pairs may not get further than Conversation 2 or 3 in the time allowed, but this does not matter. They will still have practised the core language of the topic and will not have held back the more able learners, who will have been stretched by the extra information and extra leeway to be creative, included in the later conversations.

Variations

■ Add more conversations, or extra elements to individual conversations, if more practice required, e.g. 'please take this form to the cashier at the end'; 'I'm sorry I've no large notes', etc.

■ Split the customer's and the clerk's cues between each card, so that Partner A is the customer in the first and third conversations, but is the clerk in the second and fourth, and vice versa.

■ Less information and fewer prompts can be included on the clerk's cue card in later conversations, to encourage those playing role B to remember what they need to ask and to allow them to devise their own answers to A's questions.

Activity 9 · Booking a hotel room   R12 R13

Language practised

Phrases used at a hotel reception desk, including:

Have you a (single/double/family) room?
… with bath/shower
… for … people/… nights
How much is it? (per person/per room)
Is breakfast included?

Type of activity

Pairwork, graded tasks. Roles A and B are roughly equal.

Resources

A cue card (**R13**) for each learner, one person in each pair receives an A card, the other a B card.

Preparation

Demonstrate a model dialogue (similar to Conversation 1 below) with the whole group. Ensure that the meaning of all the symbols is understood. Learners will gradually get accustomed to symbols if you introduce them gradually as new phrases are taught. Some symbols will be used for several different topics, such as 'for how many people?', and 'how much is it?', so learners will soon assimilate them.

See **R12** for a full set of symbols.

Procedure

1 Distribute the cue cards. Partner A plays the role of the guest and B is the receptionist. Tell learners not to look at each others' cards.

2 B begins by greeting the customer. Both partners then pursue the conversation by following the prompts on their cue cards. Remind pairs to take one prompt at a time; this will ensure that A does not merely read out all the information on the card at once at the beginning of the task and that the conversation sounds like a realistic exchange of questions and answers.

Conversation 1 (R13) will sound something like the following:

Guest:	Have you a room with a shower?
Receptionist:	For how many people?
Guest:	Two.
Receptionist:	And for how many nights?
Guest:	Two.
Receptionist:	Yes, we have.
Guest:	How much is it?
Receptionist:	£40 per person per night.
Guest:	Is breakfast included?
Receptionist:	Yes, it is.

Conversation 5 (R13), which is more complex and more open-ended and thus suitable for the stronger members of the class might sound like this:

Guest:	Have you a room with a shower?
Receptionist:	For how many people?
Guest:	Just one
Receptionist:	I'm sorry, I have got a room but it hasn't got a shower or a bath
Guest:	Oh well, I suppose that's all right. How much is it?
Receptionist:	£23 per night. How long do you want to stay?
Guest:	Four nights
Receptionist:	Oh, I'm sorry, the room is free only tonight and tomorrow, then the hotel is fully booked. If you like I could telephone another hotel and ask if they have a room for Wednesday and Thursday.
Guest:	No thank you. I'll take the room for two nights, then think about it. I'm hungry; have you a restaurant?
Receptionist:	I'm afraid the restaurant closed twenty minutes ago, but there are a few restaurants in High Street, ten minutes walk from here.
Guest:	Okay, thanks.

Variations

- Add more conversations, or elements to individual conversations, if required, e.g. where can I post a letter/send a fax/buy postcards?

- Split the guest's and the receptionist's cues between each card, so that partners take turns in playing each role. In conversation 1 Partner A is the guest, but in Conversation 2 (**R13**) he or she plays the part of the receptionist.

- Less information can be included on the receptionists' cue cards in the later conversations and they can devise their own answers and solutions to the problems.

Activity 10 · Listening to railway announcements

Language practised

Listening to language heard in railway station announcements, including numbers and times.

Type of activity

Listening comprehension, done individually.

Resources

Recording of train station announcements concerning times of trains, platforms, changes of platforms, notice of delays, etc. Most textbooks contain listening passages which can be exploited, following this model. This activity is based on the following sample transcript:

1 The train at platform 18 is the 17.47 Connex South Central to Brighton calling at Redhill, Horley, Gatwick Airport, Haywards Heath and Brighton. Please note that this train is fast to Redhill.

2 The train at platform 15 is the 17.55 Gatwick Express calling at Gatwick Airport only. Passengers are reminded that ordinary Connex South Central tickets are not valid on this service.

3 The train at platform 19 is the delayed 17.22 to Bognor Regis calling at East Croydon, Redhill, Three Bridges, Crawley, Ifield, Littlehaven and Bognor Regis. Connex South Central apologise for the delay; this was due to the late arrival of the incoming train. Hurry along, please, the train is now ready to depart.

4 The train at Platform 16 is the 18.04 to Reigate calling at Clapham Junction, East Croydon, Purley, Redhill, where the train will divide, and Reigate. Passengers for Reigate should travel in the front four coaches.

You will also need one blank grid per learner:

Platform	Time	Destination	Additional information

Preparation

Numbers and the 24-hour clock should be revised before playing the tape. As this is a listening **comprehension** exercise, learners need to hear a variety of times and numbers several times, rather than produce them themselves. Dictate a list of times and have learners write down the times in figures. If you have a weak group, include times in your list that appear on the tape recording.

For extra practice of times, and to make a change from just writing them down, give each learner or each pair of learners a toy clock with moveable hands. These can often be picked up cheaply from jumble sales or you can make them easily and cheaply with a paper plate and a paper fastener. You say a time and learners have to turn the clock hands to that time. Add an element of competition if you wish, seeing who can get the right answer first.

Procedure

1 Give each learner a copy of the grid on the previous page.

2 Play the tape several times, pausing briefly between each announcement. Tell your class you will play the tape three or four times (depending on how you think they will cope and how much language they will be able to assimilate on each listening).

3 After listening for the first time (or first and second time), learners can fill in the first two columns; after the second (or third) listening they can fill in the third column and after the final listening they can try and fill in the right-hand column.

4 When finished, the most able learners' tables might look like this:

Platform	Time	Destination	Additional information
18	17.47	Brighton	Fast to Redhill
15	17.55	Gatwick Airport	Non-stop; Connex South Central tickets not valid
19	17.22	Bognor Regis	Delayed; train about to depart
16	18.04	Reigate	Train divides at Redhill; passengers for Reigate travel in front 4 coaches

Of course, even after three or four listenings weaker learners might only have filled in the first couple of columns, while the more able might have filled in most of the required information after hearing the tape just once. But in this activity, based on a grid where each column is graded in difficulty, each person in the class is working at his or her own pace and level. No-one knows how well or badly anyone else is doing, so no-one can feel embarrassed at seeming to be 'behind'.

5 To check the activity, put up a completed grid on the OHP and play the tape one more time for people to be able to check where they went wrong.

Variations

■ Hand out partially completed grids, particularly if there are town names which learners may not have heard of.

- Hand out the answers as well (perhaps including a few red herrings) but not in the right order, to help weaker learners. Those that don't need the support don't have to look at the answers!

- Many listening passages in course books lend themselves to this type of exploitation. Look out for passages which contain three or four pieces of information about a number of items, some facts being short and direct, e.g. in a 'shopping' passage these might include colour, size and price but with other information given in longer sentences, using more complex vocabulary and structures, e.g. having presents gift-wrapped, asking to try things on, saying why the item is unsuitable, etc.

Activity 11 · Elvis Presley

R14

Language practised

The past tense
Years
When did … ?
What happened in … ?

Type of activity

Pairwork for learners of the same or different ability (depending on how the information given is split between the role cards). See tutor preparation below.

Resources

The tutor needs to select a list of facts about someone's life. Any person's details can be used, fictional or real, celebrity or not; this is a good opportunity for learners to find out more about a figure from their target country, e.g. Goethe, de Gaulle, Sophia Loren, etc. Below are some facts about the life of Elvis Presley.

1935	Elvis Presley born
1953	left school, became a lorry driver
1955	met his manager, Colonel Tom Parker
1956	recorded 'Heartbreak Hotel'
1958	joined the army
1960	left the army
1967	married Priscilla Beaulieu
1973	divorced
1977	Elvis Presley died

The information above needs to be split between two cue cards A and B for distribution to the learners. If the partners are unevenly matched by ability, give partner A (the weaker) a list containing all the information. Partner B (the stronger of the two, or the person who needs most practice in using numbers) receives a cue card with the years only. See Variations below for how to produce cue cards for pairs of equal ability.

Preparation

This activity is suitable for a class where the past tense and/or years have been taught or practised during the lesson.

Ask learners when they were born, got married, got divorced, met their spouse, joined the army (or the language class).

For more practice of years, have a quiz where you supply a list of events and learners try and remember when they happened. Supply the answers, but jumble up the years. The class can work in two or three teams if the questions and years are written on handouts. Include a mixture of events that are easy to remember and those that are difficult. To make it more difficult include only events in the last forty or fifty years or so. Include vocabulary which also appears during the Elvis activity. Suitable events are:

- the end of the war;

- the death of Marilyn Monroe;

- the assassination of President Kennedy;

- the marriage of Prince Charles;

- the birth of Prince Harry;

- the election of Boris Yeltsin as President of Russia.

However, it is good to link the events to the country where the language you are teaching is spoken, as well as to the age and interests of your learners.

Ensure you have oral feedback and checking of answers, so that learners actually get the opportunity to speak the years, not just write them.

Procedure

1 Partner B asks 'What happened in 1956?', etc. Partner A replies 'Elvis recorded 'Heartbreak Hotel' and so on.

2 Partner B writes in the event.

3 A and B check their cards against each other or there is a class feedback session.

Variations

- For intensive practice of forming questions Partner A receives a cue card containing all the information concerning Elvis as in the tutor's list above. Partner B (the stronger of the two) receives a cue card containing only the phrases about Elvis Presley without the dates. Partner B asks 'When was Elvis born?', 'When did Elvis get divorced?', etc, thus he or she has to form sentences in the past tense; Partner A can read off the year.

- If the pairs are evenly matched by ability, each partner can receive some years and some facts on a grid, the aim being to plug the information gap and fill in all the blank spaces in the grid, as below. See **R14** for French, German and Spanish worksheets.

1935	Elvis Presley born
1953	
1955	met his manager, Colonel Tom Parker
1956	recorded 'Heartbreak Hotel'
1958	
1960	left the army
	married Priscilla Beaulieu
1973	
1977	Elvis Presley died

1953	Elvis Presley born
1955	left school, became a lorry driver
1956	
1958	joined the army
1967	left the army
	married Priscilla Beaulieu
1973	divorced
	Elvis Presley died

- One partner has only the dates on his or her cue card; the other has only the facts (or, alternatively, both partners can have a cue card containing all the information, but with the years not attached to a particular event). Together the students have to discuss when they think each event happened, e.g.:

Partner A: When did Elvis join the army?

Partner B: Well, I suppose he was about 18. He must have been born in 1935, because that's the earliest date on the card. He was 18 in 1953, so I think he joined the army in 1953.

Partner A: Yes, but he left school and became a lorry driver before joining the army, so I think he must have left school in 1953. Did he have any hits before he joined the army?

Partner B: Yes, I think so, because he was quite famous by the time he became a soldier. I think he had already recorded 'Heartbreak Hotel', so he must have joined the army in 1956 or 1958. What do you think?

… and so on. This activity is really quite challenging and allows good students plenty of opportunity for interaction.

- For another more challenging task, replace the verbs in the biography with nouns, so that learners themselves have to think of the correct verb and put it into the past tense, e.g.:

1955   first meeting with manager, Colonel Tom Parker
1967   marriage to Priscilla Beaulieu

44   Other ideas

- There is no reason why different pairs in the class should not be doing different variations of the activity at the same time, in which case each pair is given slightly different role cards. They are all talking about Elvis Presley, reading exactly the same information but using different levels of language.

- Months and dates can be added to the years for extra practice.

Activity 12 · Where is it?

R15

Language practised

Where is …?
Prepositions – on, under, on top of, on the right hand side of, to the left of, behind, etc.
Dative case after prepositions (German): *auf, unter, neben, an, hinter, über.*

Type of activity

Pairwork, suitable for partners of unequal ability.

Resources

Cue card A and cue card B (**R15**).

Preparation

Practise putting classroom objects in different places to practise all the different prepositions you intend using. The tutor can ask the question 'where is the bag?' and learners reply.

The only problem with the above is that it can get boring; everyone can see where the bag is so it seems pointless to ask. To avoid this and turn the activity into a more realistic and meaningful one, hide a variety of different objects around the room before the class arrives – in the desk drawer, behind the filing cabinet, under the chair, etc. Pretend you have lost your bag, your pen or whatever and ask 'where's my bag? does anyone know?' Learners will start offering various possibilities – is it in your car/ under the desk?, etc.

If learners need more practice, you can turn the activity into a sort of party game where one person goes out of the room and the rest of the class hides a particular object. The person who has been outside has the more difficult task, i.e. asking 'is it behind the curtain/ in someone's pocket, etc. Ask for volunteers to avoid embarrassing weaker learners.

Procedure

1 Distribute the cue cards so that one partner (the stronger) is A, the other B. It is important that they do not look at each others' cards.

2 Explain that B has to draw in the objects, based on A's explanation.

3 B begins by asking 'where is the computer?' and so on until he or she has drawn in all eight items.

4 When the activity is finished, the pair can compare pictures.

Variations

■ This activity uses vocabulary found in an office so is good for a business language class. Any context for the picture can be chosen and any items included.

Activity 13 • Ordering a drink in a café   R16

Language practised

Je voudrais ...
Avez-vous ...? /est-ce que vous avez ...?
Donnez-moi ...
Ça coûte combien?

Type of activity

Pairwork, suitable for partners of unequal ability.

Resources

Cue card (**R16**). In the example given both roles are on the same card, but they can be split, if preferred.

Preparation

Vocabulary for drinks will have been taught this lesson. Combine the practice with the phrases '*je voudrais*' and '*avez-vous?*'. You can use flashcards or real bottles, packets, etc to illustrate the items, but it is also a good idea to have a flashcard showing the symbols that you have used on the cue card, just in case they are unclear.

If learners are not familiar with this style of exercise, where symbols and arrows are used, go through an example with the whole group, before turning to pairwork. The example you work through can be the same as in the cue card or can differ slightly – perhaps include tea and coffee instead of champagne. You need not say very much, just point to the symbols and elicit their meaning. Symbols for various drinks are needed in this activity. See **R16** for a set of symbols.

46

If words are used on role-play cards, learners tend to stick rigidly to the actual words used, which inhibits fluency. Symbols mean that learners can respond using language that is suitable for the context and with which they can cope. In most languages there are several phrases which are more or less synonymous, but are just of varying levels of difficulty. If students see the English phrase 'how much do I owe you?' on a cue card, they may well try and translate the word 'owe' and have difficulty coming up with the correct expression in the target language. If, instead, they see the symbol FF (see left) they might say *'Je vous dois combien?'*, if they can remember it, but if they can't, then expressions like *'ça fait combien?'* or *'c'est combien?'* are just as appropriate to the context and keep the conversation flowing. The drawing of a table will be interpreted as *'est-ce que vous avez une table?'* by some students, *'vous avez une table libre?'* by others, another student might offer *'j'ai reservé une table'* while a very weak student might just say *'une table, s'il vous plaît'*. All of these expressions are suitable for the given situation and would be understood by a waiter in a French restaurant.

Another way of rehearsing the activity to ensure that everyone carries out the pairwork activity properly, is to have two strong learners demonstrate the dialogue (from the OHT) in front of the class.

Procedure

1 Distribute one cue card (**R16**) per pair.

2 One learner takes the role of the waiter and the other the customer. They produce a dialogue based on the symbols on the cue card. One pair's dialogue might sound like this:

Customer:	Bonsoir.
Waiter:	Bonsoir, monsieur.
Customer:	Est-ce que vous avez une table?
Waiter:	Pour combien de personnes?
Customer:	Deux.
Waiter:	Oui, voilà.
Customer:	Le menu, s'il vous plaît.
Waiter:	Voilà, monsieur.
Customer:	Le champagne, c'est combien?
Waiter:	200 FF, monsieur.
Customer:	Une bouteille, s'il vous plaît.
Waiter:	Oui, monsieur.

Using exactly the same cue card, a stronger or more adventurous pair's dialogue might sound like this:

Customer:	Bonsoir.
Waiter:	Bonsoir, monsieur. Je peux vous aider?
Customer:	Est-ce que vous avez une table?
Waiter:	Pour combien de personnes?
Customer:	Nous sommes deux.
Waiter:	Je vais voir, ah oui, il y a une table là-bas dans le coin. Venez avec moi, monsieur.
Customer:	Voulez-vous nous donner le menu, s'il vous plaît.
Waiter:	Oui, tout de suite, monsieur.
Customer:	Le champagne, c'est combien?
Waiter:	Une bouteille coûte 200 FF, monsieur.
Customer:	Alors, je vais prendre une bouteille, s'il vous plaît.
Waiter:	Oui, monsieur. C'est tout?

3 When learners have finished, they can swap roles and change some of the items ordered. You can hand out more role cards, draw more symbols under the dialogue outline, numbering them 2, 3, 4, etc to show that these are the items to be ordered in later conversations, or just leave it to the learners' imaginations.

Variations

■ If both partners are of a similar ability add more symbols to the waiter's half of the dialogue to give him or her more to say. For instance, the customer could order two or three items at first, none of which is available. Eventually he or she asks 'what have you got?' (symbolised by just a question mark); at this point the waiter's symbol shows a variety of different drinks not yet mentioned. His cue card can also prompt him to recommend various drinks.

47

Activity 14 • Chain drill

Language practised

Here, times, but this activity is easily adaptable to practise any grammar point or vocabulary.

Type of activity

Whole class.

Resources

None.

Preparation

This activity should follow the presentation of times on the clock, when you feel that learners are ready for practice, but in a controlled setting where you can keep an eye out for those who are still having difficulty.

Ideally the group should sit in a circle or horseshoe shape.

Procedure

1 Explain the rules of the activity: each person repeats the information others have given, while adding on a phrase.

2 The tutor or a learner can begin by saying '*je me lève à 8 heures*'.

3 The next person says, '*John se lève à 8 heures, moi, je me lève à 8 heures moins le quart*'.

4 The next person says, '*John se lève à 8 heures, Meera se lève à 8 heures moins le quart et moi, je me lève à sept heures et demie*'. Learners carry on for as long as they are able.

5 Learners may offer any time they wish, if they are still unsure of how to express 'a quarter to' or 'twenty past' they can just say a simple phrase such as '*à 7 heures*'. In other words, everyone can join in at their own level.

6 An element of competition can be brought in – anyone who forgets what was said beforehand is out, resulting in a winner. Alternatively, as someone says a time, write it up on the board, showing that the activity is aimed at maximising oral practice, rather than a memory test.

Variations

■ This is a variation on the traditional English party game *My grandmother went to market*, which goes as follows:

First player:	My grandmother went to market and bought some apples.
Second player:	My grandmother went to market and bought some apples and four lemons.
Third player:	My grandmother went to market and bought some apples, four lemons and a watermelon.
Fourth player:	My grandmother went to market and bought some apples, four lemons, a watermelon and some potatoes

... and so on. The 'add-on' concept can be used for almost any grammatical point, as well as the fruit and vegetable vocabulary being practised above, for instance:

Verbs:

First person:	*Le samedi je joue au golf.*
Second person:	*Le samedi je joue au golf et vais au supermarché.*
Third person:	*Le samedi je joue au golf , je vais au supermarché et je nettoie ma voiture* ... and so on.

Accusative case:

First person:	*Ich möchte einen schwarzen Mantel.*
Second person:	*Ich möchte einen schwarzen Mantel und eine grüne Jacke.*
Third person:	*Ich möchte einen schwarzen Mantel, eine grüne Jacke und ein weißes Hemd* ... and so on.

Direct object:

First person:	*Maria compró un ramo de flores.*
Second person:	*Maria compró un ramo de flores y una bolsa de caramelos.*
Third person:	*Maria compró un ramo de flores, una bolsa de caramelos y una chocolatina* ... and so on.

Activity 15 • Exploiting a listening text

Language practised

Here, the language needed when shopping, and names of fruits, but this will depend on the text chosen.

Type of activity

Class will usually listen to the tape as a whole group but fill in their worksheets or answer the questions at their own level (differentiation by outcome).

Resources

Recording, question sheet, any support material, e.g. vocabulary, the answers in jumbled up form.

Preparation

Do not play the tape 'cold', but have a warm-up session to elicit vocabulary that may appear on the tape. For the following example, flashcards can be shown to remind learners of the names of fruits (**R9**). You can also ask 'What do you say when you go into a greengrocer's shop?', 'do you prefer red or green apples?', etc. It is, thus, important to be familiar with the tape content so that you can anticipate any difficulties and pre-teach them.

Play the tape at least once before handing out worksheets, answer grids, etc. If you give out handouts first, learners will read them instead of listening to the tape.

The first time you play the conversation, you can play it through without stopping, but when learners are expected to answer questions, make frequent use of the pause button.

Finish off by playing the tape through one more time without stopping. Weaker learners will have one more chance of answering questions, while stronger learners will have a chance to check their work.

Procedure

Play the tape, following the guidelines above. The following is the transcript of a typical dialogue at beginners' level:

Shop Assistant:	Can I help you?
Customer:	A pound of apples, please.
Shop Assistant:	Red or green?
Customer:	Red ones, please. Oh, and a pound of bananas.
Shop Assistant:	I'm sorry, we've sold out of bananas.
Customer:	Never mind, can I have six lemons please.
Shop Assistant:	I'm afraid we've only got five left.
Customer:	I'll just take those then.
Shop Assistant:	Anything else? The plums are lovely today.
Customer:	No, my children don't like plums very much. That's all for today, thank you. How much do I owe you?
Shop Assistant	That's £1.45 please.

Vendeur:	Je peux vous aider?
Cliente:	Un kilo de pommes, s'il vous plaît.
Vendeur:	Des pommes rouges ou vertes?
Cliente:	Des rouges, s'il vous plaît. Ben, et un kilo de bananes.
Vendeur:	Désolé, je n'ai plus de bananes.
Cliente:	Tant pis. Alors, je voudrais six citrons, s'il vous plaît.
Vendeur:	Il nous en reste seulement cinq.
Cliente:	Bon, je les prends.
Vendeur:	Et avec ceci? Les prunes sont délicieuses aujourd'hui.
Cliente:	Non, merci. Mes enfants n'aiment pas tellement les prunes. C'est tout. Je vous dois combien?
Vendeur:	22 francs, s'il vous plaît.

Different ways to exploit the text

■ Ticking certain words.

> **Tick the words as you hear them:**
>
> ☐ lemons ☐ apples
>
> ☐ plums ☐ bananas

■ Put items in order.

> **Put the following items in the order in which they were mentioned on tape:**
>
> ☐ lemons ☐ apples
>
> ☐ plums ☐ bananas

■ Ticking only specified items

In this activity, unlike in the first two, students have to actually understand the text. All the words are spoken on tape, but not all refer to items that were actually bought.

> **Tick those items that the customer bought:**
>
> ☐ lemons ☐ apples
>
> ☐ plums ☐ bananas

■ Yes/no questions.

> **Answer the following questions with Yes or No:**
>
> The customer buys a pound of apples. **Yes | No**
>
> The customer buys a pound of bananas. **Yes | No**
>
> The customer wants five lemons. **Yes | No**
>
> The customer's children don't like plums. **Yes | No**

■ True or false questions.

> **Say whether the following statements are true or false:**
>
> The customer buys a pound of apples. **True | False**
>
> The customer buys a pound of bananas. **True | False**
>
> The customer wants five lemons. **True | False**
>
> The customer's children don't like plums. **True | False**

■ Multiple choice questions.

> **Which of the following is correct:**
>
> 1 ☐ a the customer wants red apples.
>
> ☐ b the customer wants green apples.
>
> ☐ c the customer does not want apples.
>
> 2 ☐ a the total cost is 45 pence.
>
> ☐ b the total cost is £1.45.
>
> ☐ c the total cost is £2.45.

■ Matching.

> **Match up the phrases in the left-hand column with the correct phrase in the right-hand column:**
>
> The customer buys a pound of   plums
>
> The customer's children don't like   lemons
>
> The shop has sold out of   apples
>
> There are only five   bananas

■ Gap filling.

If desired, the vocabulary to be used can be given at the bottom of the page, but in a different order. The less able learners may appreciate this.

> **Fill in the blanks:**
>
> Shop Assistant: Can I help you?
>
> Customer: A _____ of _____, please.
>
> Shop Assistant: Red or green?
>
> Customer: _____ ones, please. Oh, and a pound of _____.
>
> Shop Assistant: I'm sorry, we've sold out of _____.
>
> Customer: Never mind, can I have _____ lemons, please.
>
> Shop Assistant: I'm afraid we've only got _____ left.
>
> Customer: I'll just _____ those then.
>
> Shop Assistant: Anything else? The plums are _____ today.
>
> Customer: No, my _____ don't like plums very much. That's all for today, thank you. How much do I owe you?
>
> Shop Assistant   That's _____, please.

■ Correcting deliberate errors.

> **Rephrase the statements correctly:**
>
> The customer buys a kilo of apples.
>
> _____
>
> The shop has sold out of apples.
>
> _____
>
> The customer buys six lemons.
>
> _____
>
> The lemons are lovely today.
>
> _____

■ Short answers.

> • What kind of apples does the customer buy?
> • How many lemons does she buy?
> • What has the shop sold out of?
> • What are lovely today?

■ Longer answers to open questions.

> • Why doesn't the customer buy bananas?
> • Why can't she buy six lemons?
> • Why isn't she interested in the plums?

- Summary.

    Summarise the content of the dialogue.

- Grid response.

    After the first listening learners fill in the first column, after the second listening they fill in the second column, after the third listening they fill in the third column and those who can also fill in the fourth column.

Item	Mentioned?	Available?	Quantity bought	Other information
Apples				
Bananas				
Peaches				
Lemons				
Melons				
Plums				

In mixed-ability classes it is usually the case that one type of activity is not suitable for the whole class. Ideally different learners should be given different activities depending on their level. However, this is not always practical in a class of adults, as a tutor will probably offend sensitive learners if he or she is perceived as treating them differently from others in the class.

One way around the problem is to give each learner a worksheet containing three or four different tasks of varying difficulty (e.g. blank filling, answering in the target language, multiple choice), and giving them a choice of which questions to answer – the most able can do the whole lot if they want. At least in this case no-one knows which level questions everyone else is answering; as far as an observer is concerned, all students will be seen to be writing answers. See **R17** for a worksheet in French.

The grid-type activity is particularly useful for mixed-ability classes, because it contains so many different tasks within the one exercise (listening for certain words as well as understanding the meaning). What happens in practice with a graded grid like this is that the more able learners fill in several columns after just one listening, while the less able are still concentrating on the first columns even after hearing the tape several times. As long as you do not pick on a weaker learner when going through the answers at the feedback stage, no-one need feel embarrassed at not completing the lot, as no-one else will know who has done what. You can always say at the start of the activity that the final column is difficult and learners aren't expected to fill it in completely; then, if anyone does manage to get some information, they will feel proud of themselves.

Chapter 6: Consolidation activities

Activity 16 • Arranging to meet

Language practised

Qu'est-ce que vous faites (lundi soir)?   *Vous êtes libre …?*

Voulez-vous …?   *Si on allait …?*

Je voudrais …   *Je préférerais …*

Je ne peux pas   *Je suis occupé(e)*

Je dois …

Type of activity

Pairwork, suitable for partners of similar ability.

Resources

Cue card A and cue card B (see **R19**).

Preparation

Before letting learners work in pairs, ensure that they have had plenty of practice of both inviting someone to do something and also accepting or turning down an invitation.

To elicit '*Voulez-vous … aller au théâtre; … dîner avec moi; … jouer au badminton*', have a number of flashcards or symbols on an OHT indicating an activity (see **R18**).

Restrict your role at this stage to just holding up a card or pointing to a diagram, while each learner produces an invitation to a different place or to do a different activity. To ensure that learners use the language to be used during the pairwork activity, flashcards can include vocabulary mentioned in the role cards. Revise days of the week at the same time by asking learners to specify a day.

As learners start producing the language of invitations fluently, ask individuals to reply. You can nod or shake your head to indicate to a learner how to reply. When you shake your head, a flashcard can be held up again, so that learners use that in their reply – '*Non, je ne peux pas, je vais au théâtre*'. Shake your head more often than you nod it as in this activity learners will need to refuse most invitations. Hold up yet another flashcard again to prompt learners to say '*je préférerais …*'.

Procedure

1   Distribute the cue cards so that one partner is A, the other B. Tell them not to look at each other's card.

2   Set the context: in this telephone conversation you are trying to find a convenient time one evening next week to play badminton with your partner. You both usually work till about 5pm. Using your 'diary', i.e. cue card, negotiate a mutually convenient time.

3   Suggest that A begins.

Variations

■ To differentiate by text: where ability levels are unequal, give the weaker partner an 'easier' cue card. Perhaps include more information on the diary to provide more support – the verb to be used can be given, for instance – *aller au spectacle,* or limit the activities chosen to only those that can be used with *aller,* e.g. Glasgow, *théâtre, restaurant.*

■ To differentiate by interest: include activities relevant to your group. If you have a class of business people change the context, e.g. learners are trying to find a suitable time for a meeting, and fill the diaries with appropriate activities, e.g. *visite à la nouvelle usine, conférence, rendez-vous avec un client.*

Activity 17 · Lost children

R20

Language practised

Describing a person's appearance, e.g: he's got short, dark hair;
she's small with long, blonde hair, etc;
describing what someone is wearing:
he's wearing a light checked shirt;
she's wearing a plain skirt, etc.

Type of activity

Pairwork, suitable for partners of similar ability. This is a 'differentiated by text' activity, so each pair can be given cue cards at an appropriate level.

Resources

Cue card A and cue card B (see **R20**). If possible, use different cards for each pair. This means that you can choose which set of cards to give to each pair (and some will be easier than others). Also, as pairs finish, they can swap with another couple, or you can hand them another set of cue cards.

To broaden the language practised to include colours, you can make similar cards very easily at home using coloured photographs found in home shopping catalogues. You will need two identical catalogues, so that your 'lost child' can appear on both cards, if wished.

Preparation

This activity is suited to a lesson where you have been teaching description of appearance (if it is an elementary class), or more complex clothes items and description (e.g. ribbons, trainers, striped, plain, spotted, woollen, etc).

During the practice phase of the lesson learners might have described each other or people in a magazine.

Try and ensure that any unusual vocabulary on the cue cards (pigtails, braces or whatever) is either mentioned orally, or listed in vocabulary given out on a handout. However, you do not need to worry if not every item of clothing in the pictures is known, as the children are distinguishable from each other in several respects.

You must be very familiar with your cards, so that you know which are 'easier' or 'harder' than others. Hand a set at the appropriate level to each pair, without making it obvious that they are graded.

Procedure

1 Set the scene. One partner (A) plays the role of a distraught parent who has lost his or her child in a large department store, the other person (B) plays a 'supervisor of lost children' at the store. The children on B's card are all the currently 'lost children'.

2 A and B imagine they are talking on the phone, with A describing what his or her child looks like and B searching through the pictures on his or her cue card to see if he or she has that child.

3 If A does not offer enough information, B should ask questions to establish which child is meant.

4 When B is sure that he or she has the child, he or she can check with A by pointing to the child and saying 'is this your daughter/son?'. If other groups are still working, or you want learners to have more practice, give the pair another set of cue cards.

Variations

■ Partners can also be paired one strong and one weak. In this case, the stronger one tends to do most of the talking, regardless of which role he or she is playing. If playing the role of the parent he or she will tend to describe the child without waiting for questions from B, who will merely listen and check the description against the drawings he or she has. If playing the role of the supervisor, the stronger partner will probably ask lots of questions – 'is it a boy or a girl?', 'how old is he?', 'what's she wearing?', 'has she got long or short hair?', etc.

■ By making your own cue cards, you can limit the language to a few key expressions on some cards, or you can make cue cards more complex for stronger pairs. If you look at the three sets of cue cards illustrated, you will notice that the top set is the easiest of the three illustrated, as the children are all dressed in different garments and plain colours and are easily distinguishable from each other. In fact, once you've established it's a boy, you can eliminate three of the pictures immediately. The middle set is more difficult and will require more detailed questioning and information, since the children are all dressed rather similarly, so things like shoes and hairstyle will need to be taken into account. The bottom set will lead to a very long discussion as A's child is not actually on B's card, although very similar looking children are.

55

Activity 18 • Ordering in a restaurant

R21

Language practised

Food vocabulary.
Je voudrais ...
Est-ce que vous avez ...?
Qu'est-ce que vous avez ...?
Donnez-moi ...

Other language structures may also be practised, if they are highlighted before the activity

Type of activity

Pairwork, or groups of three or four. This is a 'differentiated by text' activity, so each pair or group can be given a cue card at the appropriate level

Resources

A menu (**R21**) for each group. It is more interesting and realistic if real menus are used. You may have amassed a collection of authentic menus from the target country. These vary in the amount of difficult vocabulary and information they contain and if learners are working on role plays involving ordering a meal in a restaurant, weaker groups can be handed a simple menu, with fewer choices and known vocabulary, whereas a more able group can handle a more sophisticated menu. If you hand out the real thing rather than photocopies, learners will not feel they are being singled out for special treatment; no-one would expect you to have a dozen or more copies of the same menu.

Preparation

Have a sample menu on OHT or flashcards and practise ordering items from it in the practice phase of the lesson. The tutor can play the role of the waiter (the less difficult role).

Work through a model conversation based on symbols (see Activity 13, p45), to encourage learners to use a variety of phrases, e.g.:

> *Qu'est-ce que vous avez comme boissons?*
> *Non, je ne mange pas de viande.*
> *C'est quel parfum?*
> *Qu'est-ce que vous avez comme dessert?*   or whatever you want them to practise.

Procedure

1 Hand out one of the menus per group. Match the menu to the ability level.

2 Set the context, e.g. you are ordering a meal for yourself and your friend, ask about drinks and price.

3 The waiter can begin by greeting the customer(s).

Variations

Make the context more specific, imposing restrictions, which will encourage learners to ask more questions and read the menu more carefully. Learners playing the role of customer may be handed a little card telling them what they should take into consideration when ordering, e.g:

■ You are a vegetarian (encourages learners to ask whether a dish contains meat).

■ You are allergic to tomatoes (encourages learners to ask what is in each dish).

■ You are on a diet (encourages learners to ask what is in each dish).

■ You do not want to spend more than 200 FF overall (encourages learner to read an à la carte menu and possibly 'order' something unusual).

■ You want a traditional meal.

■ You don't like mushrooms.

■ You want something cold.

> *Vous êtes végétarien (nne).*
> *Vous êtes allergique aux tomates.*
> *Vous êtes au régime.*
> *Vous ne voulez pas dépenser plus de 200 FF en tout.*
> *Vous voulez un repas traditionnel.*
> *Vous n'aimez pas les champignons.*
> *Vous voulez un repas froid.*

If pairs or groups are uneven as regards ability, let a weak learner play the role of the waiter, who can get away with saying just a few set phrases, e.g. *Vous désirez, monsieur? C'est tout?*

Activity 19 • Sound effects

Language practised

Present and/or past tense.

Link words, such as then, afterwards, a few minutes later, *puis, ensuite, après ça, quelques minutes après.*

Any context is possible, just choose sound effects accordingly. If you wish to practise extensively a specific grammar point, say, reflexive verbs, include sounds which, when 'translated into words' require reflexives, for instance the sound of someone brushing their teeth or waking up or the sound of a door opening. Other grammatical structures can be stressed, provided that you make it clear to the group first that this is what you want, e.g. sentences of the type: *après avoir fait quelque chose, il a ... (fait quelque chose d'autre),* or the passive voice.

Type of activity

Small group activity (three or four people per group). It does not matter how the groups are split – by random would be a good choice – as everyone can offer suggestions at their own level. This is a very open-ended activity, so caters for different interests and personalities as well as different abilities.

Resources

A tape of sound effects (or use a ready-made one – try the EFL shelves of a bookshop).

Preparation

Make a note of what is on the tape, e.g. telephone ringing, heavy rain, glass breaking, etc so that the vocabulary can be revised or pre-taught in the warm-up period. If you make up your own tape, you can use the vocabulary you consider important and leave out anything which may be beyond the students' capabilities or be rather obscure, e.g. sneezing, snoring, braying, etc.

Procedure

1 Play the tape to the whole class, eliciting the vocabulary for the sounds by asking 'What's that?' or 'What's happening here?'. It is usually possible to conduct this phase in the target language; most people will recognise a baby crying or a door creaking when they hear it, translation won't be necessary.

2 Remind learners to jot down the sounds in the order they appear on the tape, so that they will be able to remember what to include in their story.

3 The class then gets into small groups and each group thinks up a story line to match the sound effects. The object of the activity, to use the foreign language as much as possible, so do not object if groups depart from what is on the tape or come up with implausible stories.

4 If wished, stipulate any criteria learners are to follow; you might suggest a punch line that must be the final sentence of the story, or you might give a vague expectation of the type of story you want – the hero is Xavier Roman, a detective, for example – or indicate an opening phrase.

5 After a set amount of time (say 15–20 minutes) let each group read or act out their story to the other groups. One person can act as spokesperson for the group, or each can contribute to the narrative. In this way, shyer learners do not to need to speak more than they feel comfortable with.

Activity 20 • Picture stories

Language practised

The language of description – of a landscape, portrait or event.

Reasons **why** you like, dislike or have chosen something.

Any language can be practised, just choose appropriate pictures. For instance, if you want to practise the past tense, choose pictures which contain lots of action, so that learners can imagine a narrative.

Pictures of people provide opportunity to practise the language of supposing or guessing, e.g. 'I suppose she has just been …', 'I think they are going to …', 'he looks as if he might …'

Type of activity

During the first phase of the activity learners work individually. This is followed by pair- or small-group work (three or four per group).

Resources

A number of postcards or pictures (see **R22** – could also be works of art or just advertisements cut from Sunday supplements). The pictures should depict a variety of subjects and themes, e.g. the peaceful countryside, a bustling market, buildings, portraits, a winter scene – nothing but summer landscapes or only battle scenes will not make for such imaginative and varied stories. Have at least as many pictures as there are learners in the group, but the more you have the better, as learners can choose something to their taste.

Preparation

Learners each choose one picture. If you wish, you can tell them in advance what the task will be, as this will undoubtedly affect their choice, e.g. describing what is on the card or saying what you like about the picture you have chosen. Occasionally, however, do not give them any information about the task to come, just spring a surprise on them and allow their imaginations free rein, e.g. the task is to imagine what happens next.

Procedure

1 Tell learners what they are to do with their picture, if you have not already told them. Possible tasks, as well as those mentioned above, might be:

> Why is he or she smiling? (for a portrait)
> What made you choose that picture?
> What are the people in the picture talking about? Imagine their conversation.

2 Learners work individually on the task you set for five or ten minutes. Wander round helping anyone who needs it.

3 When the time is up, learners take it in turn to tell the rest of the group about their picture. Write up on the board and comment on any key vocabulary as it arises.

4 In the second phase of the activity, learners get into small groups, taking their pictures with them. While learners have been working individually (see step 2), you decide how the group should be split. Group composition will depend on the pictures that have been chosen – ideally a group will include one portrait (the hero of the story?) and at least one background scene or concrete event/activity. There is no right or wrong combination, and if there are only tenuous connections between the pictures and the story line, it does not matter. The pictures act merely as stimuli to discussion.

58

5 Set the new, group task. Learners are to make up a story, based on the pictures in sequence which can be as simple or as fanciful as they like. They combine their pictures and together work on a story line. If you wish you can specify limiting criteria, e.g. the story must contain a hero, or there must be two heroes, a man and a woman, or the story must be about disappointment. This group preparation can last about fifteen minutes.

6 Each group now feeds back their story to the rest of the class, holding up their pictures as appropriate. One person can act as spokesperson for the group, or each can contribute to the narrative. In this way, shyer learners do not to need to speak more than they feel comfortable with.

Variations

- Pictures can be chosen to suit learners' interests or to include particular language. Each picture might include a different sporting activity, or might depict a different type of weather and season.

- Pictures might be chosen with a view to leading on to another discussion. For instance, all the pictures you choose might be by French impressionists, which might provide background information for a reading or listening comprehension you plan to do in a future lesson. Learners can be exposed to vocabulary now, which may come up again in the near future.

- You can talk about a topic related to the target language country, e.g. say Irish artists, to your class, improving their overall cultural knowledge as well as their foreign language skills.

59

Activity 21 · Board game

R23 R24

Language practised

Passé composé and forming questions (here). The same format can be used to practise any language – merely substitute different cards

Type of activity

Small group – three or four people, similar ability.

Resources

One 'board' per group (could be a large photocopied sheet of paper – see **R23**), one die per group, a counter for each group member, four piles of small cards, each involving a different type of task (see **R24**).

Preparation

Decide what language points you wish learners to practise and prepare ten or twelve little cards for each point. You will find it easier to set up the game if you use a different colour for each pile of cards (the sample board given in **R23** uses patterns, instead of colour – after photocopying, it would be a good idea to colour these squares using different coloured highlighter pens).

The tasks could be:

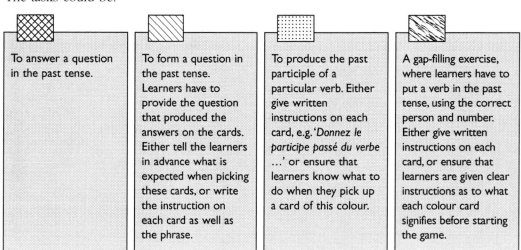

| To answer a question in the past tense. | To form a question in the past tense. Learners have to provide the question that produced the answers on the cards. Either tell the learners in advance what is expected when picking these cards, or write the instruction on each card as well as the phrase. | To produce the past participle of a particular verb. Either give written instructions on each card, e.g. 'Donnez le participe passé du verbe …' or ensure that learners know what to do when they pick up a card of this colour. | A gap-filling exercise, where learners have to put a verb in the past tense, using the correct person and number. Either give written instructions on each card, or ensure that learners are given clear instructions as to what each colour card signifies before starting the game. |

Set the board up for each group, putting the colour-coded piles of cards in the centre of the board.

Procedure

1 All group members start with their counters at the beginning.

2 The first player throws the die and moves as many spaces around the board as the die indicates.

3 If players land on a white (i.e. unpatterned) square, they do nothing and play continues, with the next person throwing the die. If players land on a coloured (or patterned) square they must pick up a small card of the same colour or pattern and do the task demanded by the card.

4 If the task is completed successfully (i.e. the whole group is satisfied that the correct answer has been given) the person who has just performed the task has another go (or, if you prefer, the rules can be that play passes to the next person without any second turns).

5 The game finishes when the first person arrives at ⊻.

Variations

- Boards can be devised with more or fewer colour-coded squares. There should, however, be enough for learners to have to perform at least two or three tasks per game, otherwise the game will lose its language-learning purpose.

- If more colour-coded squares are added to the board, you do not have to think of different categories of task. The same colour and hence the same type of task can be used more than once.

- A more competitive spirit can be brought to the game by making players miss a turn if they do not get the French right on first attempt – however, do not try this unless all group members are thick-skinned and self-confident.

- Tasks can be devised to suit the level of the class. If the class is very mixed ability, ensure that small group members are of a similar ability to each other and give each group different sets of cards geared to their different levels. One (weaker) group could have the question: 'Vous avez regardé la télévision ou écouté la radio ce matin?' while a stronger group's question could read … 'Nommez deux choses que vous avez faites ce matin.'

- This format can be used to practise any language point, or to be a general revision or 'fun' exercise. For instance, for vocabulary practice one pile of cards could ask learners to 'name ten things you would find in a bathroom', 'name ten fruits', etc.

Part 3
Photocopiable resources

61

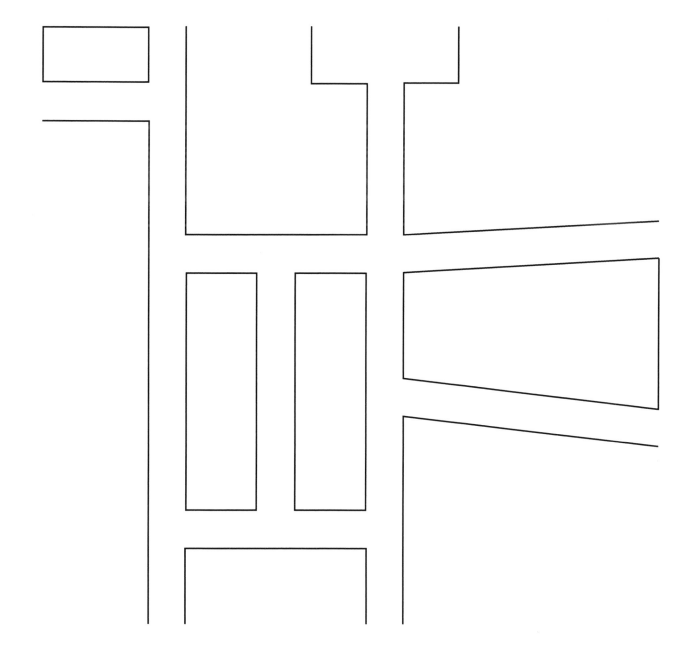

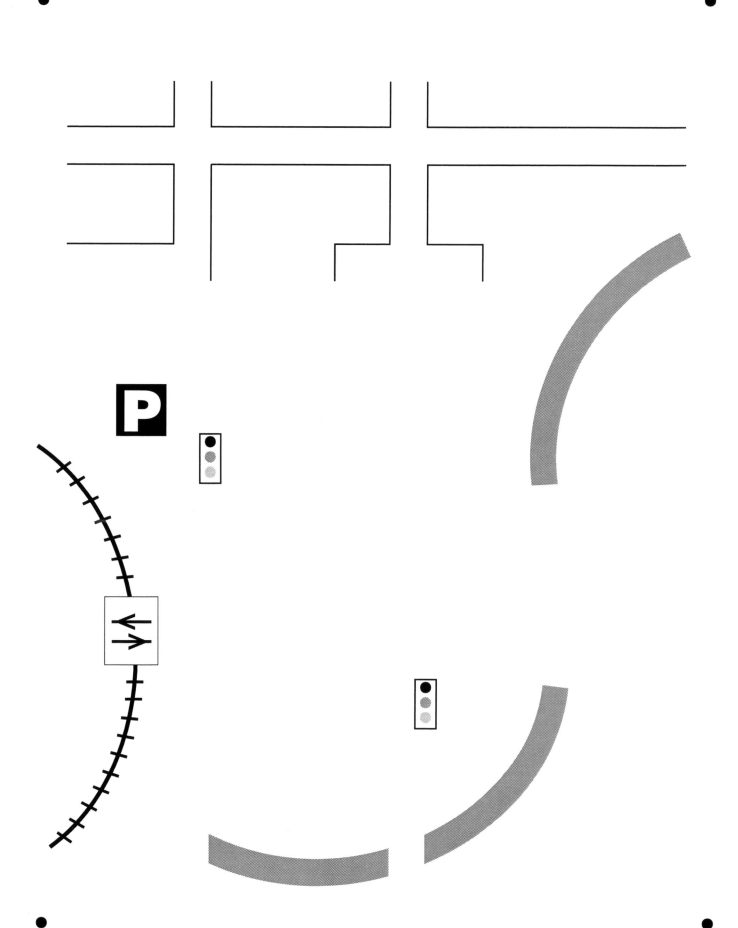

mixed-ability teaching in language learning

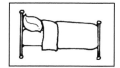

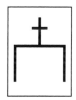

x

x

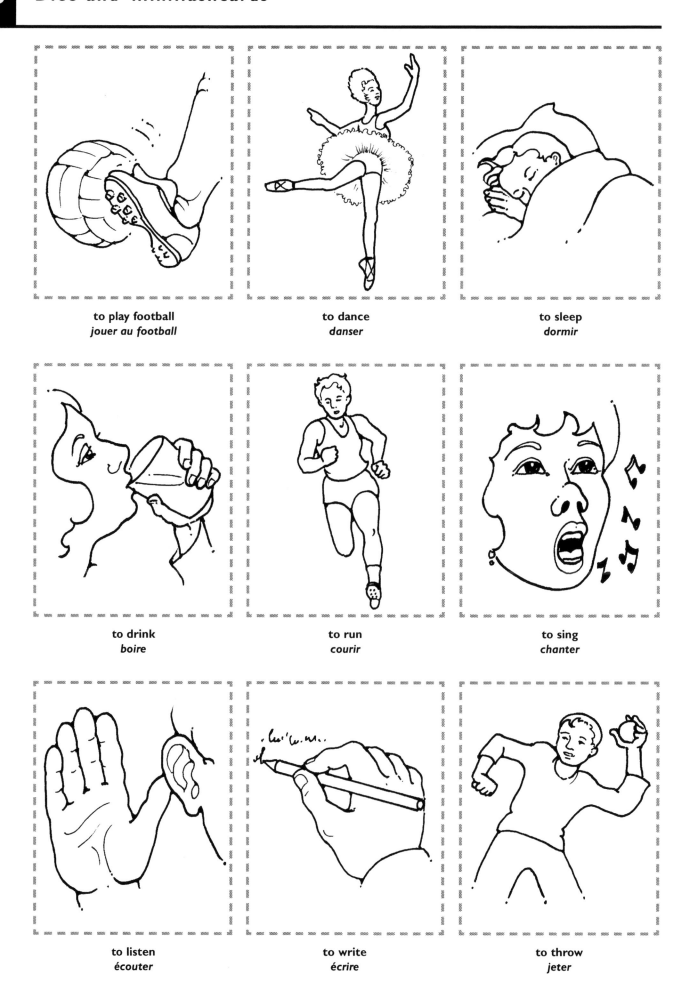

to play football
jouer au football

to dance
danser

to sleep
dormir

to drink
boire

to run
courir

to sing
chanter

to listen
écouter

to write
écrire

to throw
jeter

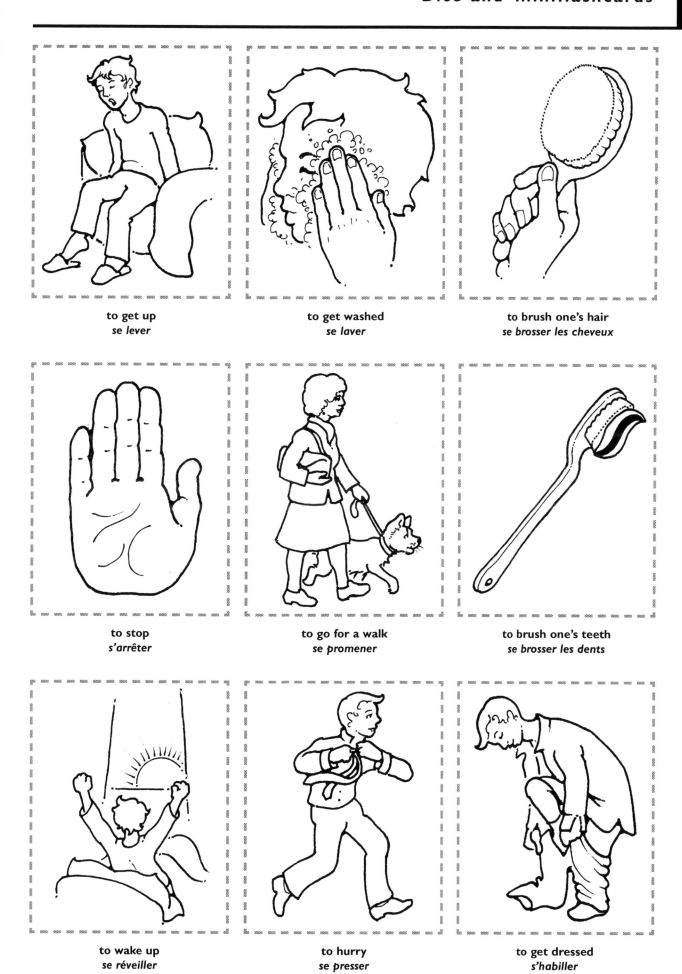

to get up
se lever

to get washed
se laver

to brush one's hair
se brosser les cheveux

to stop
s'arrêter

to go for a walk
se promener

to brush one's teeth
se brosser les dents

to wake up
se réveiller

to hurry
se presser

to get dressed
s'habiller

mixed-ability teaching in language learning   **69**

A

Nom . . . .

Prénom . . . .

Date de naissance . . . .

Nationalité . . . .

Adresse en France . . . .

Raison du séjour en France . . . .

Durée du séjour en France . . . .

B

Vadim Chevchenko	Yoko Ito	Helen Janssen
Né le 23.3.1978	Née le 9.6.1955	Née le 1.10.1963
Russe	Japonaise	Sud-africaine
Faculté de microbiologie, Université de Grenoble	L'hôtel Bristol, Nice	L'hôtel Ibis
Une année	Assister à une conférence	Fille étudie à la Sorbonne
	5 jours	2 semaines

A

Nachname ....

Vorname ....

Geburtsdatum ....

Nationalität ....

Adresse in Deutschland ....

Grund des Aufenthalts in Deutschland ....

Länge des Aufenthalts in Deutschland ....

B

Vadim Chevchenko	Yoko Ito	Helen Janssen
Geb. 23.3.1978	Geb. 9.6.1955	Geb. 1.10.1963
Russe	Japanerin	Süd-Afrikanerin
Medizinische Fakultät, Universität Köln	Hotel am Stadtpark, Bonn	Hotel Meridien
Ein Jahr	Anwesenheit auf einer Konferenz	Tochter studiert an der Universität München
	Fünf Tage	Zwei Wochen

A

Nombre ....

Apellido ....

Fecha de nacimiento ....

Nacionalidad ....

Dirección en España ....

Razón de su estancia en España ....

Duración de su estancia en España ....

B

Vadim Chevchenko	Juan González	Abigail Smith
Fecha de nacimiento: 23.3.1978	Fecha de nacimiento: 9.6.1955	Fecha de nacimiento: 1.10.1963
Ruso	Argentino	Americana
Facultad de derecho, Universidad Autónoma de Madrid	Hotel NH	Casa de Huéspedes
Tres meses	Para asistir a una conferencia	Viajando por Europa
	Cuatro días	Dos meses

soupe aux légumes	yaourt aux cerises	lait	jambon
Gemüsesuppe	Kirschjoghurt	Milch	Schinken
sopa de verduras	yogurt de cerezas	leche	jamón

champignons	tomates	confiture de fraises	pommes de terre
Pilze	Tomaten	Erdbeerkonfitüre	Kartoffeln
champiñones	tomates	mermelada de fresa	patatas

bananes	carottes	beurre	fromage
Bananen	Karotten	Butter	Käse
plátanos	zanahorias	mantequilla	queso

A

Tomates (1kg)	Tomaten (1kg)	Tomates (1kg)
Champignons (100g)	Pilze (100gm)	Champiñones (100gm)
Lait (1l)	Milch (1l)	Leche (1l)
Pommes de terre (3kg)	Kartoffeln (3kg)	Patatas (3kg)

B

Confiture de fraises (un pot)	Erdbeerkonfitüre (eine Dose)	Mermelada de fresa (1 tarro)
Yaourt aux cerises (un pot)	Kirschjoghurt (ein Stück)	Yogurt de cerezas (1 unidad)
Jambon (4 tranches)	Schinken (4 Scheiben)	Jamón (4 lonchas)
Soupe aux légumes (1 boîte)	Gemüsesuppe (1 Dose)	Sopa de verduras (1 lata)

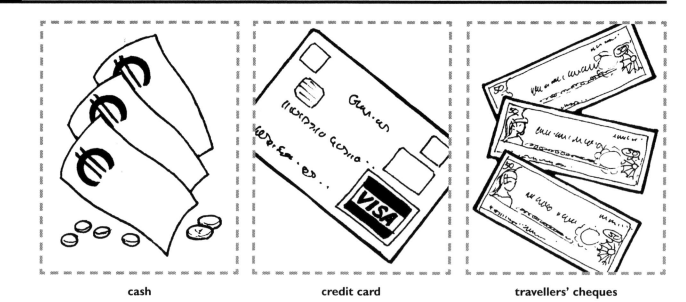

cash

credit card

travellers' cheques

signature

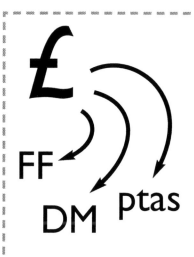

change Pound Sterling to ...

£10 = ?

€5 = ?

$20 = ?

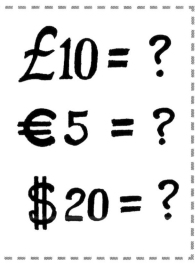

what denomination notes?

percentage commission

rate of exchange

passport

mixed-ability teaching in language learning

A **B**

1

$100 → £

£? $?

= 1.56

2

$60 → £

$60 → £ [VISA card]

£? $?

= 1.62

[signature]

3

DM200 → £ [notes]

£? $?

£10 + £5

%

= 2.92

how?

= 1%

4

£ → 950FF [VISA card]

£? $?

%

✗ [passport]

= 8.78

= 1%

?

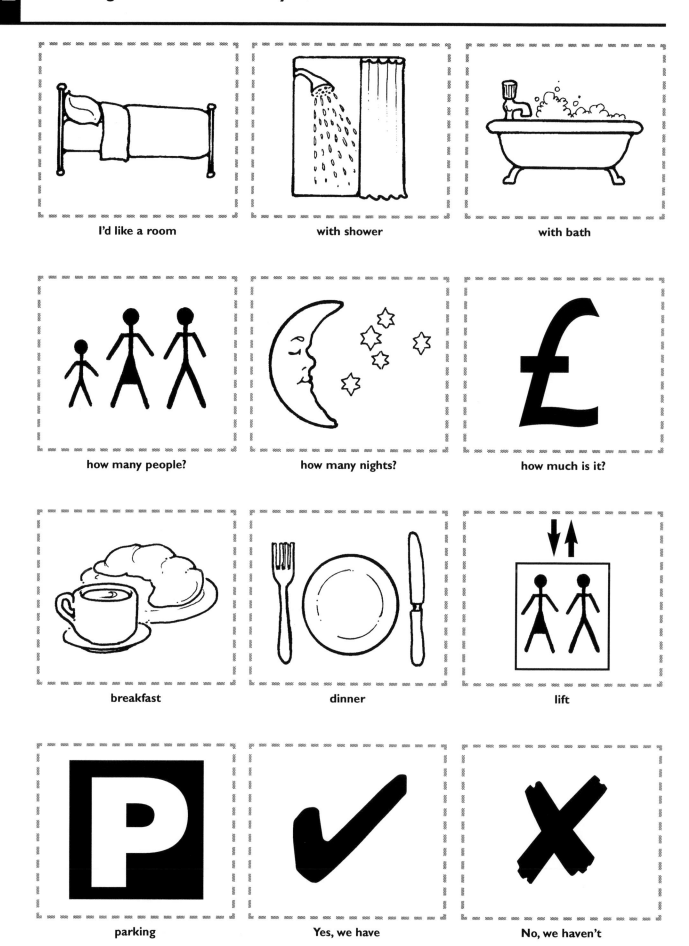

I'd like a room

with shower

with bath

how many people?

how many nights?

how much is it?

breakfast

dinner

lift

parking

Yes, we have

No, we haven't

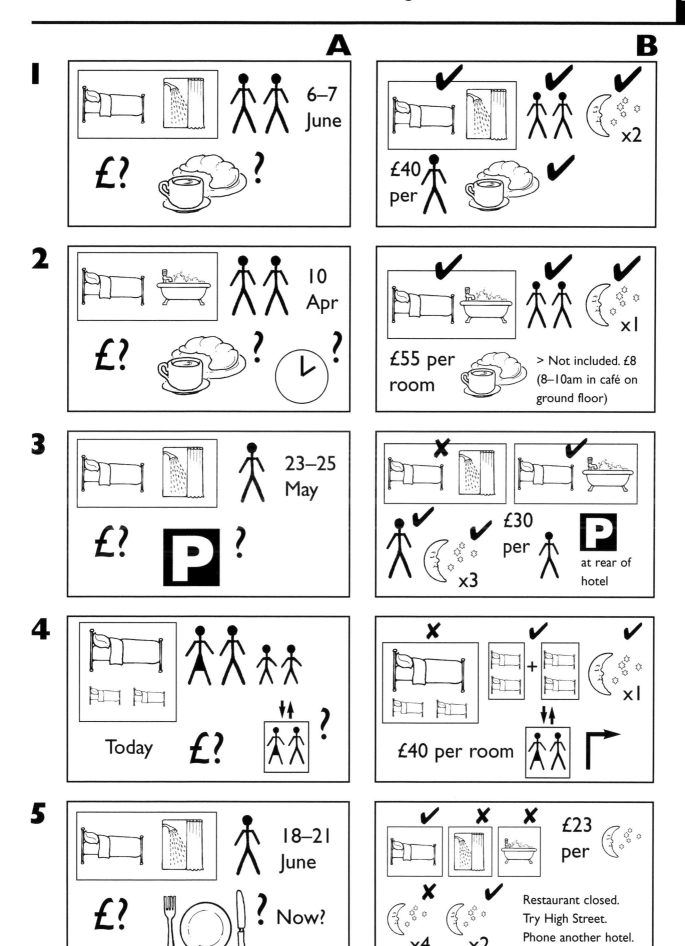

A

1890	de Gaulle est né à Lille
1916	
1940	
1944	les Puissances alliées ont libéré la France
1947	
1959	est devenu Président de la Cinquième République
1965	
1968	manifestations violentes et grèves en France
1969	a donné sa démission comme Président
1970	

1749	Goethe ist in Frankfurt-am-Main geboren
1768	
1774	hat *Die Leiden des jungen Werthers* geschrieben
1775	ist nach Weimar umgezogen
1786	
1791	ist Direktor des Herzogstheaters in Weimar geworden
1794	
1806	
1808	der erste Teil von *Faust* ist herausgebracht worden
1832	

1943	nace Julio Iglesias en Madrid, España
1959	es expulsado del coro de su colegio en Madrid
1969	
1971	
1975	nace su tercer hijo Enrique Iglesias Preysler
1979	
1985	
1989	es nombrado representate especial de las artes de UNICEF
1992	
2000	graba un nuevo album titulado 'Noche de cuatro lunas'

B

1890	
1916	s'est battu dans la bataille de Verdun
1940	s'est échappé de la France occupée, est allé en Angleterre
1944	
1947	a établi un nouveau mouvement politique 'Le Rassemblement du Peuple Français'
1959	
1965	a gagné les élections présidentielles pour la deuxième fois
1968	
1969	
1970	est mort

1749	
1768	hat das Jurastudium an der Leipziger Universität beendet
1774	
1775	
1786	ist nach Italien gefahren
1791	
1794	hat Friedrich von Schiller kennengelernt
1806	hat Christiane Vulpius geheiratet
1808	
1832	ist gestorben

1943	
1959	
1969	graba su primer album en Londres
1971	se casa con la filipina Isabel Preysler
1975	
1979	su matrimonio con Isabel Preysler queda anulado
1985	recibe una estrella en el camino de la fama de Hollywood
1989	
1992	su album 'Calor' sale en español, francés, portugues, alemán e italiano
2000	

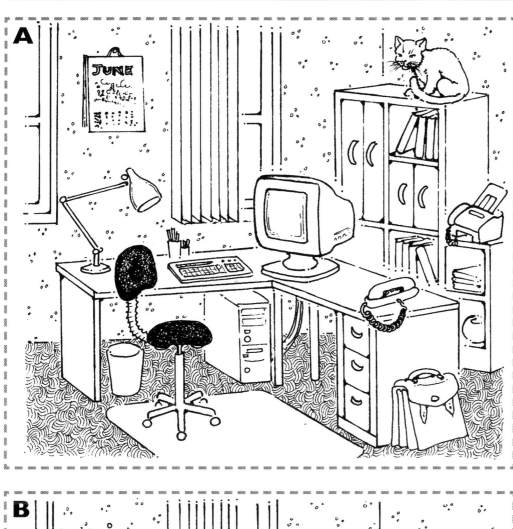

A

B

l'ordinateur
der Computer
el ordenador

le télécopieur
das Faxgerät
el fax

le téléphone
das Telefon
el teléfono

la lampe
die Lampe
la lámpara

la chaise
der Stuhl
la silla

le calendrier
der Kalender
el calendario

le porte-documents
die Mappe
la cartera

le chat
die Katze
el gato

good evening

table

have you got?

how much is it?

champagne

wine

coffee

menu

customer   waiter

**Cochez les fruits
que vous entendez:**

☐ des citrons

☐ des prunes

☐ des pommes

☐ des bananes

**Cochez les fruits
qu'elle achète:**

☐ des citrons

☐ des prunes

☐ des pommes

☐ des bananes

Vendeur: Je peux vous aider?

Cliente: Un ...... de ...., s'il vous plaît.

Vendeur: Des pommes rouges ou vertes?

Cliente: Des ...., s'il vous plaît. Ben, et un kilo de ....

Vendeur: Désolé, je n'ai plus de ....

Cliente: Tant pis. Alors, je voudrais ...... citrons, s'il vous plaît.

Vendeur: Il nous en reste seulement ....

Cliente: Bon, je les ....

Vendeur: Et avec ceci? Les prunes sont .... aujourd'hui.

Cliente: Non, merci. Mes .... n'aiment pas tellement les prunes.
            C'est tout. Je vous dois combien?

Vendeur: ...... francs, s'il vous plaît.

La cliente, pourquoi est-ce qu'elle n'achète pas de bananes?

Pourquoi est-ce qu'elle n'achète pas six citrons?

Pourquoi est-ce qu'elle ne veut pas de prunes?

go to the theatre

have dinner

play badminton

watch a football match

play golf

go shopping

go to the park

go to an exhibition

go to the cinema

mixed-ability teaching in language learning

A

LUNDI	
MARDI	19h, spectacle 'Bugsy Malone' à l'école
MERCREDI	terminer le travail à 13h
JEUDI	
VENDREDI	20h, excursion au théâtre avec le club

MONTAG	
DIENSTAG	19 Uhr Musical Bugsy Malone, Schule
MITTWOCH	Arbeitsschluss – 13 Uhr
DONNERSTAG	
FREITAG	20 Uhr Theater mit Club

LUNES	
MARTES	A las 19:00 horas el espectáculo 'Bugsy Malone' en el colegio
MIÉRCOLES	Termina el trabajo a las 13:00 horas
JUEVES	
VIERNES	A las 20:00 horas teatro con club

B

LUNDI	20h, dîner avec Boris
MARDI	
MERCREDI	voyage d'affaires à Glasgow, retour à 22h30
JEUDI	
VENDREDI	17h, rendez-vous chez l'opticien

MONTAG	20 Uhr Abendessen mit Boris
DIENSTAG	
MITTWOCH	Geschäftsreise nach Glasgow, Rückkehr um 22 Uhr 30
DONNERSTAG	
FREITAG	17 Uhr Termin beim Optiker

LUNES	A las 20:00 horas cena con Boris
MARTES	
MIÉRCOLES	viaje de trabajo a Glasgow, regreso a las 22:30 horas
JUEVES	
VIERNES	A las 17:00 horas cita con el oculista

A

B

Chez Nico

Assiette de charcuterie
Salade de tomates
Soupe à l'oignon

Escalope de veau
Omelette jambon ou fromage
Coq au vin

Mousse au chocolat
Crème caramel
Glace

l'ange gourmand

ENTREES
Salade niçoise	70 F
Bouillabaisse	65 F
Pâté maison	60 F
Cocktail d'avocat	60 F

PLATS
Boeuf à la provençale	115 F
Côte d'agneau	125 F
Escalope de dinde	95 F
Sole meunière	95 F
Cassoulet	85 F

DESSERTS
Sorbets	50 F
Profiteroles	65 F
Pâtisserie maison	55 F
Glace (3 parfums au choix)	50 F

Café des théâtres

Terrine du chef

Crudités

Melon glacé

∞

Navarin d'agneau

Poulet aux frites ou riz

Truite aux amandes

Couscous Marrakech

∞

Ile flottante

Glace

Tarte aux pommes

1
2

23	24

21		27
20		28
		29
18	34	
17	33	31
16		8

| 4 |
| 5 |
| 6 |

| 13 | 12 | | 9 |

Qu'est-ce que vous avez mangé ce matin?	Est-ce que vous avez jamais goûté des escargots?	A quelle heure êtes-vous arrivé(e) à l'institut ce soir?
Est-ce que vous êtes resté(e) à la maison hier soir ou est-ce que vous êtes sorti(e)?	Qu'est-ce que vous avez regardé à la télévision hier soir?	Qu'est-ce que vous avez fait hier soir?

J'ai bu du café.	Nous sommes allé(e)s en Espagne.	Non, j'ai regardé la télévision.
Je suis venu(e) en voiture.	J'y suis allé(e) avec ma femme/ mon mari.	Rien.

dormir	faire	venir
recevoir	avoir	prendre

Qu'est-ce que vous **(faire)** pendant les vacances?	Tu **(voir)** le nouveau film de Brad Pitt?	Nous **(rester)** dans un très bon hôtel.
Les étudiants n' **(entendre)** pas le professeur.	Je n' **(être)** aux Etats-Unis	J' **(avoir)** mal à la tête hier.

Appendix 1: A lesson plan

Language introduced

The future tense.

Other language practised: the language of making suggestions and invitations; days of the week and times.

Do not introduce both verb structures in the same lesson. It is likely that learners are already quite familiar with the language of making suggestions and invitations, e.g: let's, would you like to ...?, *voulez-vous* ...?, *möchten Sie* ...?

English: I will be ... or I'll be ...; where will you be ...? Shall we ... (go/meet/visit, etc)? Let's ...

French: *Je serai; où serez-vous? Voulez-vous ... (aller/visiter, etc)? Si on ... (allait/visitait, etc)?*

German: *Ich werde ... sein; wo werden Sie sein? Möchten Sie ... (gehen/sehen, etc)? Wollen wir ... (uns treffen/gehen, etc)?*

Level

Intermediate, although if the future tense is straightforward in your language this lesson might be suitable towards the end of the first year.

Learning objective

By the end of the session learners will be able to say where they will be (i.e. use the future tense of the verb 'to be'). They will also be able to arrange to meet someone.

Duration

A two-hour session is assumed, with the first 30 minutes given over to administrative matters, marking homework, revision and social chat.

Resources needed

OHT showing next week's 'diary' (see below).

Flashcards (see p90) with names of towns written on them or picture postcards representing a variety of towns (can be in the country of the target language if you wish but they can be any easily recognisable town);

Grid if wished, although learners can also just draw columns in their notebooks.

MONDAY	*Edinburgh*
TUESDAY	*Leeds*
WEDNESDAY	*Liverpool*
THURSDAY	*Exeter*
FRIDAY	*Birmingham*

Presentation of future tense (5 mins)

Set the scene by saying something like: 'I'm very busy; I have a lot of work; Next week I'm travelling on business.'

Show either the grid (see p89) or the map on the right or devise similar OHTs using towns relevant to your target language. To make it absolutely clear that you are referring to the future you can add next week's dates to the OHT (Monday 14, Tuesday 15, etc).

Mon 14 > Edinburgh

Tues 15 > Leeds

Wed 16 > Liverpool

Fri 18 > B'ham

Thurs 17 > Exeter

Point to the OHT and say: 'On Monday I'll be in Edinburgh', 'On Tuesday I'll be in Leeds' and so on through all the days.

This is a fairly straightforward language structure and these five sentences will probably be enough for the initial presentation phase.

Controlled practice of the future tense (10–15 mins)

You now want to see if the learners have grasped the 'will be' form and can use it themselves. Keep the OHT on show and hold up a flashcard showing the name of a city:

Manchester   *Glasgow*

or:

have names of towns written on small pieces of paper which are put in a 'hat', then let each learner pick one;

or:

distribute picture postcards which depict a well-known town (e.g. pictures of the Eiffel Tower, Statue of Liberty, St. Basil's Cathedral, etc);

or:

ask learners to draw up a make-believe diary for themselves for next week, copying your model on the OHT but using any towns they wish.

Continue as follows:

Tutor: On Monday I'll be in Edinburgh. Where will you be?
Learner 1: I'll be in Brighton.
Tutor: On Wednesday I'll be in Liverpool. Where will you be?
Learner 2: I'll be in Berlin.

Note that in the early stages the form that learners must use (I'll be) is included in your question – all learners have to do is copy you. After a few examples of this type, drop the first half of your question and just ask various learners:

Where will you be on Thursday, Meera?
Where will you be on Friday, Sid?

Eventually drop the verb form from this question, too, and just ask:

And you, Lee?
What about you, Sarah?

If learners produce the correct form, you can assume they have assimilated the new structure. They cannot be just imitating you, as you are not including the future form in your question.

Learners have not yet practised the 'you' form, so you could have a quick chain drill.

Learner 1 (turns to neighbour): On Monday I'll be in Madrid. Where will you be?
Learner 2: I'll be in Istanbul. (Turns to neighbour) Where will you be on Wednesday?
Learner 3: I'll be in Dublin. (Turns to neighbour) Where will you be on Tuesday?

… and so on.

Presentation (or revision) of making arrangements to meet (25–30 mins)

Now you want an answer from a learner which matches 'your' diary. Either give one learner the name of one of the towns written on the OHT, e.g. Birmingham, and say 'Where will you be on Friday?' or switch off the OHP and contrive it so that when one learner replies 'On Tuesday I'll be in Vladivostok', you hold up a piece of card with the same town on and say: 'Really? I'll be in (Birmingham/Vladivostok) too. Shall we meet?'

Often, if you pause before saying 'shall we meet?', and look pleased and/or surprised, someone in the group will make the suggestion first. If the correct language structure is not used, e.g. someone pipes up with 'go together' or 'you can meet', you can pretend to be pleasantly surprised as you say: 'Yes, that's a good idea, shall we meet?'

The conversation might go as follows:

Tutor:	Shall we meet?
Learner:	Yes, okay
Tutor:	What shall we do?
Learner	(maybe prompted from others in the class): Go to the cinema.
Tutor:	Yes, shall we go to the cinema? What time shall we meet?
Learner:	Seven o'clock?
Tutor:	Yes, okay, let's meet at 7 o'clock. Where shall we meet?
Learner:	At the hotel?
Tutor:	Yes, good idea. Let's meet at 7 o'clock at the hotel.

Brainstorm other suggestions for a meeting, using a variety of different verbs. Prompt suggestions by holding up the names or pictures of towns again. Insist that learners begin by saying 'shall we …?' or 'let's …'. You will receive suggestions such as:

■ have dinner together;

■ visit the Louvre;

■ go to a football match;

■ go sightseeing;

■ have a ride in a gondola.

Learners can work at their own level by making their suggestions as simple or as difficult as they can manage. As suggestions are made, write a selection up on the board, making clear how the structure is built up:

Shall we	go to the theatre
Let's	go sightseeing
	have dinner
	visit a museum

Brainstorm all the ways of answering a request, and write the ones that you consider most useful on the board (or have them already printed on a handout). Start with how to accept:

■ Yes, I'd love to.

■ That's a good idea.

■ That would be nice/lovely.

■ Okay.

■ Yes, let's.

Let learners question each other across the classroom. One learner makes a suggestion: 'Shall we go to a nightclub?' And the learner to whom the question was referred replies: 'Yes, okay'.

To add a bit of interest and relate the activity more to the target country, you can specify a town before each suggestion. Learners have to think of a suitable activity for that town.

Tutor:	Madrid
Learner 1:	Shall we go for a paella?
Learner 2:	Yes, I'd love to.
Tutor:	Toronto
Learner 3:	Shall we watch an ice-hockey match?
Learner 4:	Yes, that's a good idea.
Tutor:	Edinburgh
Learner 5:	Let's visit the castle
Learner 6:	Yes, let's.

After a few minutes of this, move on to eliciting ways of turning down a request, together with any suitable excuses. Write key phrases on the board.

■ I'm sorry, I can't. I'm busy/ I've got too much work/ I've got another appointment.

■ Oh dear, I'm afraid/that's rather difficult.

■ I'd prefer to ...

■ I'd rather ...

Again, let learners make suggestions to one another across the classroom, but this time the second person has to turn down the request. Weaker or less confident class members can respond with a simple excuse, while the more able, more imaginative or more confident learners can make an alternative suggestion.

Learner 1:	Shall we go to the opera on Friday?
Weaker learner 2:	I'm sorry, I can't, I'm busy on Friday.
Stronger learner 3:	Oh dear, what a shame, I'm busy on Friday. Are you free on Saturday? Shall we go on Saturday?
Stronger learner 4:	I'm afraid I'm not very keen on opera. I'd rather go to the cinema.

If you feel that more practice is needed, a short pairwork activity can be included at this point. The use of cue cards (see **R19**) will ensure that learners concentrate more on the language of making, accepting and refusing suggestions than on spending a lot of time thinking up the words for unusual activities.

Pairwork activity (5 mins)

Make a cue card depicting six activities for each class member. Tell them to tick three activities, which they would like to do, and put a cross against the other three, to denote things that they do not want to do. They must not show their ticks and crosses to their partner.

One person makes a suggestion or invites his or her partner to do something, using the symbols on the card as prompts: 'Shall we go to a restaurant tonight?' The other partner agrees if he or she has ticked that activity: 'Oh yes, I'd love to, thanks' or refuses if that activity is crossed: 'I'm sorry, I'm afraid I can't, I'm on a diet.'

Stronger learners will probably want to add more – by suggesting another activity, or by expanding the conversation to talk about which restaurant. The core activity is making the suggestion and accepting or turning it down simply, so all learners will cover this language.

The activity continues with each person making a suggestion until all six activities have been covered or until you decide to stop the activity because most of the class have finished.

Before starting the free activity, practise the 'shall we meet?' form. Hold up flashcards or point to symbols representing various places (see **R18**). Begin by asking the question yourself:

> Where shall we meet?
> When shall we meet?

Learners can suggest a suitable answer:

> Outside the cinema
> At your hotel
> At the metro station
> In the 'King's Head' pub

Allow learners to get a chance of practising the verb form by passing a flashcard to individual students or pointing to a symbol on the OHT and indicating a learner by name. They can then either put a 'shall we' question to one of their classmates, or say 'shall we meet at 7 o'clock?' or 'shall we meet at the entrance?'.

Free activity (approx. 20–30 minutes depending on size of class)

(Based on an idea by John Langran; see 'The Russian Travelling Salesman' in *Language games and activities*', number 2 in the CILT Netword series).

Type of activity

Whole group

Preparation

Give each learner a copy of the blank grid opposite or display it on the OHP and ask learners to make a rough copy on a piece of paper.

	Mon	**Tues**	**Wed**	**Thurs**	**Fri**
Town					
Who?					
What?					
Where?					
When?					

Set the scene:

You are all in a railway carriage travelling to (target country) on business. I will use Ireland as an example. You get chatting and discover that you are all spending five days in the country and, by coincidence, are each visiting the same three towns, although not necessarily at the same time.

Now brainstorm the class for three towns in the target country and write them clearly on the board.

WATERFORD	CORK	GALWAY

Ask the class to fill in the first row of their grid by writing the town they are visiting each day. Everyone's 'itinerary' should be different, of course. One person's grid might look like this:

	Mon	Tues	Wed	Thurs	Fri
Town	Cork	Cork	Waterford	Galway	Waterford
Who?					
What?					
Where?					
When?					

Brief the group on the task. They are to find out if anyone else in the group will be in the same town on the same day. If so, they are to arrange to meet and write down the details on their grid. For instance, Sahana might discover that both she and Simon will be in Galway on Thursday, so might arrange to go to the races, meeting at 6pm in O'Reilly's Bar. After her conversation with Simon, Sahana's grid will look like this:

	Mon	Tues	Wed	Thurs	Fri
Town	Cork	Cork	Waterford	Galway	Waterford
Who?				Simon	
What?				Races	
Where?				O'Reilly's Bar	
When?				6pm	

Learners are to move from one person to another trying to fill in all the columns in their 'diary'. If they discover that they are going to be in different towns on a particular day, they should move on to another day and then on to another student.

To begin with, they will start by accepting suggestions, as they have an empty grid, but gradually, as their 'diary' fills up they will start having to turn down suggestions and suggest alternatives. Some learners will suggest that a third or fourth person join the original pair, and that is fine too.

You can stop the activity at any time. It does not matter if not all learners have completed their grid.

This activity is suitable for a mixed-ability group because it is so open-ended. Learners work at their own level, they can choose any activity, so weaker learners can stick to using language they feel comfortable with – 'go to the cinema/ theatre, etc' while the more able can be as adventurous as they are capable of. When two learners discover that they have a match, either of them can take the initiative in suggesting a place to go, so shyer or weaker learners can leave it to the more outgoing members of the group if they wish, leaving themselves only with the task of accepting or turning down the suggestion.

If you have a particularly strong group, you could try one of these variations:

■ Make it a rule that learners have to always turn down the first offer and make another suggestion. This will ensure that the language for excuses and more activity options are practised.

■ Make it a rule that learners must do something different every day. This will avoid learners taking the easy option and using the theatre or cinema for each suggestion.

If you have a weak group and feel that you want to concentrate exclusively on the future tense, just use a simplified grid made up of the top two rows only (Town and Who?). The object of this activity can be for learners to see how many other people will overlap with them, and to see if they can avoid having to be alone any day.

Feedback (5–10 mins)

When you stop the activity, gather the class together as a group and ask a general question or two such as:

Who has got a date for every day?
Who has got no free days?
Whose diary is full?
Who is busy on four days/three days?

Then ask two or three learners to tell you what they will be doing on a particular day, where they'll be, whom they will be meeting and what they will be doing.

The purpose of the feedback session is not really to continue language practice, but to let learners feel that there was a point to the activity and that you are genuinely interested in how they got on while making arrangements.

If you did notice any common errors as you were listening in on conversations during the group work, you can mention them here. Errors in the key structure (future tense) should have been mentioned to the individuals concerned during the free activity. Because of the intensive controlled practice earlier during the lesson, learners are less likely to make mistakes in the future tense form. This activity generates a lot of oral practice, albeit much of it repetitive, so there may well be some slips.

Homework

A possible oral task for homework, based on the free activity, could be for learners to prepare a short talk about their plans for their imaginary business trip using the grid they filled in during the lesson.

A similar exercise could be done in writing; let learners imagine they are writing a postcard home on the first day of their trip, saying what they will be doing when.

If it was a revision lesson and there were no new structures – perhaps there is an exam approaching and you are covering a range of structures during lessons, you could incorporate the past tense into an oral or written homework. Still using their completed grids, learners can imagine that their trip has taken place and they can talk or write a postcard about what they did over the week – where they went, whom they met and what they did.

Appendix 2: Sample questionnaire

Name _____

Language _____

Class _____ Native language _____

1 Have you ever studied the language before?   Yes   No

   If No, have you ever studied any other languages?   Yes   No

   Please give details _____

   _____

2 If you answered Yes to question 1, please give details:

   any qualifications, classes attended, other experiences, your level:

   _____

   _____

   _____

3 Why are you attending this class? What are you hoping to achieve?

   _____

   _____

4 Do you have any particular requirements?

   _____

   _____

                                        Thank you.
                                        Course tutor

Appendix 3: Resources and useful addresses

Ainslie S, Netword 3: *Mixed-ability teaching: Meeting learners' needs* (CILT, 1994) (out of print)

Ainslie S & A Lamping, Netword 4: *Assessing adult learners* (CILT, 1995)

Arthur L and S Hurd (eds), *The adult language learner* (CILT, 1992) (out of print)

Atkinson T, InfoTech 3: *WWW/The Internet* (CILT, 1998)

Convery A and D Coyle, Pathfinder 37: *Differentiation and individual learners: a guide for classroom practice* (CILT, 1999)

Fernández-Toro M, *Training learners for self-instruction* (CILT, 1999)

Hadfield J, *Elementary communication games* (Longman, 1987)

Hewer S, InfoTech 2: *Text manipulation: computer-based activities to improve knowledge and use of the target language* (CILT, 1997)

Hill B, InfoTech 4: *Video in language learning* (CILT, 1999)

Lamping A & C Ball, Netword 5: *Maintaining motivation* (CILT, 1996)

MLG Publishing Ltd, PO Box 1526, Hanwell, London W7 1ND. Tel: 020 8567 1076. Publisher of Mini Flashcards.

Tierney D & F Humphreys, ResourceFile 5: *A modern image: enhancing the use of the OHP* (CILT, 2001)

Wright, A, *1000+ pictures for teachers to copy.* Revised ed. (Longman, 1996)

97

Websites

www.bbc.co.uk/languages

www.becta.org.uk

www.becta.org.uk/linguanet

www.cheshirenetword.org.uk

www.cilt.org.uk

www.cilt.org.uk/adulteducation

www.hull.ac.uk/cti/

www.linguanet.org.uk